THOUGHTS OF AN
AMATEUR
MATHEMATICIAN

JACK McCABE

BOOKSIDE Press

Copyright © 2024 by Jack McCabe

ISBN: 978-1-77883-434-9 (Paperback)

All rights reserved. No part of this publication may be reproduced, distributed, or transmitted in any form or by any means, including photocopying, recording, or other electronic or mechanical methods, without the prior written permission of the publisher, except in the case brief quotations embodied in critical reviews and other noncommercial uses permitted by copyright law.

The views expressed in this book are solely those of the author and do not necessarily reflect the views of the publisher, and the publisher hereby disclaims any responsibility for them. Some names and identifying details in this book have been changed to protect the privacy of individuals.

BookSide Press
878-7408,090
www.booksidepress.com
orders@booksidepress.com

To the memory of Rafael Artzy and John Myhill, two mathematicians who believed that I had some talent for the subject

Acknowledgments

I worked as a teacher at the **Canterbury School** in New Milford, Connecticut. This boarding school is a community where adults and students help one another, and as such, the perfect place to support my writing.

My friend **Guy Simonelli** read the early attempt and found some math errors. He promised not to tell anyone.

Noah Blake coached me through the second version. He provided me with what I would judge to be professional-level editing. His suggestions enabled me to put together a more human story. Though not a mathematician, Noah quickly perceived the main thread of the book and helped me construct an effective sequencing of the historical events.

"Young men should prove theorems, old men should write books."
—**G. H. Hardy**

Introduction

I began my training/education as a mathematician by majoring in math at Florida State University, where I graduated in August,1961. In June, 1965, I graduated with a Masters degree in mathematics from Rutgers, The State University. I then entered a PhD degree program at SUNY Buffalo, where I completed all coursework and passed both the written preliminary and oral examinations. But, I failed to write a dissertation.

I was not confident that I could discover and prove an original theorem. I lacked the motivation required to first study others mathematicians' work and then add a small piece to the puzzle. But most importantly, I felt no passion for the subject.

After teaching math for fifty years, mostly at the high school level and a few years at the college level, I retired and began researching mathematics, focusing on the properties of natural numbers.

As an amateur, I am in good company. Historically, this company includes Pythagoras (500 BC), Euclid, (300 BC) and Pierre de Fermat, (1601-1665). These historical figures did not have any technology to aid their search, whereas today we have computers to reveal the properties of numbers.

Amateur mathematicians are not paid to discover properties of numbers. We are driven by a passionate love affair with numbers and a need to discover something true regarding the relationships of numbers.

Professional mathematicians include university professors and actuaries.

The first time I felt really excited about mathematics was when I learned how to program a computer. I had already earned both an under-graduate and graduate degree in mathematics, as well as having completed all coursework towards a PhD. Computer programming gave me the means to explore math in a way that was so different from learning from textbooks. I became an artist, teaching the computer to do all the boring stuff that is a natural part of mathematics. This process of teaching appealed to my lazy approach to doing math. I taught the computer to carry out the numerical processes that I was required to perform by hand in my earlier studies, and then the fun began.

Computer programming inspired me to ask questions and to create methods for determining possible answers, and it became my hobby. Like a woodworker or model builder, I sought out projects on which to practice my programming skills. Eventually I discovered that simple numbers held countless mysteries worthy of exploration.

The act of creating something that emerges first in the mind is a most joyful experience. Composers, writers, painters, and programmers all have this experience. "*The first requirement for programming is a passion for the work, a deep need to probe the mysterious space between human thoughts and what a machine can understand; between human desires and how machines might satisfy them.*" Those are the words of Ellen Ullman, author of "*Close to the Machine*," and best express how I felt when I discovered an algorithm necessary to teach the computer.

Reading a variety of sources led me to Pythagoras, Euclid, and Fermat, ancient mathematicians whose names I had heard, but whose works I had not studied. Two things struck me regarding their discoveries. Their interest in numbers was not prompted by any practical need, and they had no technology to aid them in their searches. They were driven by a passion to discover the logic that would reveal some hidden abstract truth about numbers. They treated numbers as mental stuff on which to ponder and with which to experiment. Learning about their discoveries gave me much joy, and a first reason to write this book.

Mathematicians have always been artists. They create proofs and sometimes they create new methods of proof. Pythagoras was the first to require proof. Three centuries later, Euclid gave us the first axioms and the method of proof-by-contradiction.

More than a millennium later, Fermat demonstrated infinite-descent, original method of reasoning.

College students who decide to major in mathematics must acquire an understanding of how one goes about proving a theorem. Revealing the various methods of mathematical proof became a second reason for writing the book. Some readers will prefer to read only the early theorems and proofs. Then, as the material gets deeper, they might read only the statement of the theorems and skip the proofs. This is understandable because reading a mathematical proof is hard work that requires patience and concentration. One must often read a proof several times to completely understand the logic being used.

Mathematics is a human endeavor, and thus the history of mathematics is a story about individual contributors. The story began long ago, so it is next to impossible to understand the daily life of Pythagoras and Euclid, and what inspired them to study the properties of numbers. Fermat, Euler, and Gauss lived after 1500 AD, so their lives are better understood. Much has been written about Kurt Godel and Paul Erdos, more recent mathematicians whom you will meet toward the end of the book. I hope the historical perspective will help readers maintain an interest in this story.

In the text I creep close to the edge of mathematical research. I have never taken a course in number theory, but I have perused some related textbooks. Many of my readers will be young and with limited mathematical maturity, so I intentionally wrote as an amateur mathematician, avoiding the esoteric language of classical number theory. As an amateur mathematician, I acknowledge my limitations. All mistakes and mathematical misunderstandings are mine. I leave it to the professional number theorists to determine if I have discovered any math of significance.

In truth, I wrote this book for me. One friend expressed such writing as "a memory dump"-- all that stuff in your head that has to find another place to reside. Just getting all this down on paper was a success for me, and the book will be a further success if it inspires some budding mathematician to discover a passion for finding some hidden truth about numbers.

"God is a child; and when he began to play, he cultivated mathematics. It is the most godly of man's games."
—**V. Erath**

Contents

Chapter One: A Passion for Natural Numbers 1
  A Passion for Natural Numbers 1
    1.2 Quotients and Remainders from Subtraction 5
    1.3 Isolating Digits in a Spreadsheet 9
    1.4 Evens as Consecutive Sums 11
    1.5 Expanding the Concept of Number 15
    1.6 Mathematical Induction 16

Chapter Two: Numbers: Friendly, Perfect, and Prime 18
  Numbers: Friendly, Perfect, and Prime 18
    2.1 Mutually Friendly Numbers 18
    2.2 Prime Numbers 20
    2.3 Decomposing a Composite Number 25
    2.4 Euclid's Search for Prime Numbers 26
    2.5 Euclid's Algorithm 28
    2.6 Euclid's Search for Perfect Numbers 29

Chapter Three: A Passion for Large Numbers 33
  A Passion for Large Numbers 33
    3.1 Fermat's Infinite Descent 33
    3.2 Fermat's Last Theorem 34
    3.3 Fermat's Search for a Formula 38
    3.4 Euler's Proof of Fermat's Little Theorem 42

    3.5 Gauss and the Prime Number Theorem *45*
Chapter Four: The Holy Grail of Mathematics 49
    The Holy Grail of Mathematics 49
        4.1 Description of a Pythagorean Box *49*
        4.2 Searching for the Holy Grail of Mathematics *52*
Chapter Five: The Unknown and the Unknowable 55
    The Unknown and the Unknowable 55
        5.1 Hilbert's Program *55*
        5.2 Goldbach's Conjectures *58*
        5.3 Gaping at Gaps *61*
        5.4 The Twin-Prime Conjecture *64*
Appendix A 70
Appendix B 71
Appendix C 72
    Adam's Algorithm *72*
Appendix D 73
    Mutually Friendly Numbers *73*
Appendix E 75
Appendix F 77
Appendix G 78
    Dedekind – Peano Axiomatic Arithmetic *78*
References 80

> *"Mathematical proofs, like diamonds, are hard and clear, and will be touched with nothing but strict reasoning."*
> —John Locke

CHAPTER ONE

A Passion for Natural Numbers

Many people admire athletes, movie stars, and musicians, but I am in awe of some mathematicians who lived centuries ago. Pythagoras, Euclid, Pierre de Fermat, Leonhard Euler, and Carl Friedrich Gauss each provided us with some creative mathematical proofs and some interesting and challenging problems to solve. They were not paid to study the properties of numbers, but did so out of a passion for finding truth. The numbers they studied are the very same numbers that children first encounter in elementary school. These natural numbers still hold secrets to be discovered. I too have developed a passion for these numbers.

Historians report that Pythagoras, who lived sometime between 600 and 500 BCE, some 300 years before Euclid, was the first academician to insist on proof. The ancient Chinese knew much about numbers and geometry, but they accepted the truth of a mathematical proposition based on examples. Before Pythagoras, examples provided sufficient evidence for the truth of a mathematical proposition.

Every example of squaring an even number results in an even number. Examples of adding an even number and an odd number always results in an odd number. But for Pythagoras and all mathematicians following him, examples are not sufficient to establish the universal truth of an arithmetical proposition.

The need for proof comes from the fact that humans sometimes guess wrong. Like the distant mirage, the proposition we see as true for so many numbers might be false for some very large number. Even one counterexample is enough to require a revision of a proposition. Our intuition can mislead us and our logic might be fallacious, resulting in mathematical errors that can lead to engineering disasters.

The story of mathematical proof has taken many centuries, and is not yet finished. But the story began with Pythagoras and it is the story I want to tell. Revealing some of the story is one of my purposes for writing this book, and in so doing I hope to help some budding mathematicians gain insight into what is meant by a mathematical proof.

Almost every proposition I write about will regard only natural numbers. The propositions are chosen to reveal the variety of ways mathematicians can reason. In the strictest sense, the proofs are not formal, but then few mathematicians ever present a formal proof. My many years as a student and teacher of mathematics have enabled me to sense what is meant by a formal mathematical proof, but I must leave its description to a more learned writer.

The first important proposition I will prove is *"If N^2 is an even number, then N is an even number."* Further on we will see how this theorem played a role in changing how the early Greeks viewed numbers. The proof of the theorem requires that I first describe how to represent even and odd numbers.

The even numbers such as 2, 4, 6, 8, etc. are the doubles of 1, 2, 3, 4, etc., so if E is an even number, it is the double of a natural number. Therefore I can represent an arbitrary even number with the expression $2J$, where J is a natural number. Since each odd number is 1 less than some even number as well as 1 more than some even number, the expression $2J-1$ or the expression $2J+1$ can be used to represent an arbitrary odd number.

I choose the expression $2J-1$ to represent an arbitrary odd number in my proof of *"An even number added to an odd number is an odd number."*

Proof: Given the even number $E=2J$ and the odd number $O=2K-$

1, the sum E+O=2J+(2K-1)=2J+2K-1=2(J+K)-1, which represents an odd number.

The next proposition will be labeled because it will be referenced further on. **Theorem A.**"*The product of two odd numbers is an odd number.*"

Proof: Given odd numbers (2J-1) and (2K-1) their product (2J-1)(2K-1) = 4JK-2K-2J+1 = 2*[(2JK)-2*(K+J)]+2*1 −1.

Since this product has the representation 2[2JK-(K+J)+1]−1, the product is an odd number.

The proposition, "*If **O** is an odd number, then **O²** is an odd number*" is true because it is an instance of **Theorem A**. The contra-positive of this proposition is the statement "If **O²** is not an odd number then **O** is not an odd number," and can be stated as **Theorem B**, "*If **N²** is an even number then N is an even number.*" This proposition is true because, from logic, the contra-positive of "P implies Q" is logically equivalent to "Not Q implies not P."

Before proving the next proposition, I need to discuss the concept of one number as a multiple of another number. The number 45 is a multiple of 3 because one can find a number such that 3 times that number is 45 (3*15=45). A number M is also a multiple of 3 if dividing M by 3 leaves no remainder. In general, a number M is a multiple of a number K, if dividing K by M leaves no remainder. The two statements "M=KQ+0 for some Q," and "M is a multiple of K" are equivalent and thus interchangeable.

I now prove "*One of any three consecutive odd numbers will be a multiple of 3.*"

Proof: The three expressions 2J-1, 2J+1, and 2J+3 together represent three consecutive odd numbers. If the first odd number is a multiple of 3, then there is nothing to prove. If the first odd number, 2J-1, is not a multiple of three, then dividing it by 3 results in one of two possible remainders, either 1 or 2. So for some quotient Q, either 2J-1=3Q+1 or 2J-1=3Q+2.

If 2J-1=3Q+1, substituting 3Q+1 for 2J-1 in the equation 2J+1=(2J-

1)+2, results in the equation $2J+1=(3Q+1)+2=3Q+3$ showing that $2J+1$ is a multiple of 3.

Likewise, if $2J-1=3Q+2$, substituting $3Q+2$ for $2J-1$ in the equation $2J+3=(2J-1)+4$, results in the equation $2J+3=(3Q+2)+4=3Q+6$, showing that $2J+3$ is a multiple of 3.

So if $2J-1$ is not a multiple of 3, then either $2J+1$ or $2J+3$ will be a multiple of 3.

These first few theorems were presented to show why representation is such a valuable method for mathematical reasoning. When mathematicians want to study a particular collection of numbers, they seek some way to represent each number in the collection. These representing expressions can be algebraically manipulated, enabling them to reach a proposed conclusion.

Many young students can look at a number and quickly determine if the number is divisible by 3. To achieve this they need only determine if the sum of the digits of the number is divisible by 3. For example, the sum of the digits of 4752 is 18 so 4752 is divisible by 3 ($4752=3*584$). But does this method always work? If so, it requires a proof.

I will use 4752 to illustrate the logic and math used in the proof of the proposition, "*If the sum of the digits of a four-digit number is divisible by 3, then the four-digit number is also divisible by 3.*" First, express 4752 as $4*1000+7*100+5*10+2$ then express this as $(4*999+4)+(7*99+7)+(5*9+5)+2$.

Rearrange this last expression to $(4*999+7*99+5*9) + (4+7+5+2)$ and express this as $(4*999+7*99+5*9) +18$. We now have $4752=3(4*333+7*33+5*3+6)$, a multiple of 3.

For a proof of the theorem in general, let abcd represent a four-digit number where the sum of the digits $a+b+c+d=3J$ for some quotient J. As in the example $abcd=a*1000+b*100+c*10+d=(a*999+a)+(b*99+b)+(c*9)+d$.

Therefore $abcd=(a*999+b*99+c*9)+(a+b+c+d)$, or $abcd=(a*999+b*99+c*9)+3J=3(a*333+b*33+3*c+J)$, a multiple of 3.

> *"The essence of mathematics is not to make simple things complicated, but to make complicated things simple."*
>
> — S. Gudder

1.2 Quotients and Remainders from Subtraction

Some years ago I became fascinated with the hidden properties of natural numbers. As I read books regarding numbers, I became aware of how often quotients and remainders come into play. In elementary school, students learn to calculate these quantities using a process called the division algorithm. As students perform short-division and long-division, they seldom realize that division can be achieved by subtraction.

To ask "How much is 28 divided by 7," is to ask "How many times can you repeatedly subtract 7 from 28 before arriving at 0?" The first subtraction of 7 from 28 yields 21, while the second subtraction yields 14. The next two subtractions yield 14–7 = 7 and 7–7 = 0, for a total of four subtractions, therefore 28 divided by 7 equals 4, a result consistent with the memorized fact that 4 times 7 equals 28.

To ask the question "How much is 30 divided by 7?" is to ask the question "How many times can you repeatedly subtract 7 from 30 before arriving at a number less than 7?" The repeated subtractions are 30–7=23, 23–7=16, 16–7=9, and 9–7=2. Four subtractions were required, so the answer is 4 times with 2 left over. The leftover 2 is called the remainder. The equation 30=4*7+2 summarizes the process and reveals the roles of the numbers 4 and 2.

A calculator can be used to find quotients and remainders. The result of entering 30/7 in my iPhone calculator is 4.28571429. Subtracting 4 gives 0.28571429 and then multiplying by 7 gives the remainder 2. Using my Texas Instruments TI-84, a much more sophisticated calculator with the integer-value function, entering int(30/7) gives the quotient 4, while entering 7*(30/7-int(30/7)) provides the remainder 2. In a spreadsheet I will use similar formulas to calculate quotients and remainders.

A spreadsheet consists of columns and rows. The columns are labeled with capital letters A, B, C, etc. and the rows are labeled with numbers 1, 2, 3, etc. The intersection of a row and a column is called a cell. Individual cells can contain numbers and text, as well as the result of calculations that use the contents of other cells.

Each individual cell has an address consisting of a letter followed by a number, which represents the column and row that intersect at that cell. For example, the cell with address C5 is the location where the third column intersects with the fifth row. Formulas that perform calculations can be expressed using the addresses of cells.

For example, placing the cursor at the cell with address C5 and entering =A5+B5 results in a sum in the cell C5. The formula =A5+B5 remains in the background while the result is seen at the location C5. If the cell A5 contains the number 17 and the cell B5 contains the number 32, then the cell C5 will contain the number 49.

	A	B	C	D	E	G	H
1							
2							
3							
4							
5	17	32	49				
6							
7							
8							
9							

Spreadsheets enable the user to view and/or review either the formulas or the calculated results. In this book, the results of the calculations of a spreadsheet are shown in the text while the results and formulas are sometimes shown in the appendix.

One of my intentions in writing this book is to illustrate the ease and power provided by electronic spreadsheets. Years ago, I explored the properties of numbers by programming a computer. There are times when the challenge requires that I do so again, but I now prefer to use a spreadsheet to explore some particular property of numbers.

Designing a spreadsheet is much like creating a computer program. Electronic spreadsheets are prevalent, and designing one does not require learning a programming language. The chart shown below is the result of my first spreadsheet, which enabled me to explore quotients and remainders.

The numbers in the first column (15, 16, etc.) are divided by the numbers in the first row (5, 6, and 7) to produce the corresponding quotients and remainders. For example, 17 divided by 5 equals 3 with remainder 2, and 17 divided by 6 equals 2 with remainder 5. The formulas used in the design of this spreadsheet can be seen in **Appendix A**.

	5		6		7		8	
	Quotient	Remainder	Quotient	Remainder	Quotient	Remainder	Quotient	Remainder
15	3	0	2	3	2	1	1	7
16	3	1	2	4	2	2	2	0
17	3	2	2	5	2	3	2	1
18	3	3	3	0	2	4	2	2
19	3	4	3	1	2	5	2	3
20	4	0	3	2	2	6	2	4
21	4	1	3	3	3	0	2	5
22	4	2	3	4	3	1	2	6
23	4	3	3	5	3	2	2	7
24	4	4	4	0	3	3	3	0
25	5	0	4	1	3	4	3	1

Look at each column of remainders and note how they occur in order. I will use this property of remainders in the proof of the next proposition.

I presented the following proposition with the students in one of my advanced high school math classes. *"The product of any three consecutive numbers is a multiple of 6."* **Hsin Yi Ho**, a student in the class, suggested that considering the possible quotients and remainders when dividing by 6 would probably lead to a general proof. As a class we collectively came up with the following results.

"The product of any three consecutive numbers is a multiple of 6."

Proof: If any one of the three consecutive numbers is a multiple of 6, then so is their product. For example, given the three consecutive numbers 41, 42, and 43, we see that 42=6*7, so the product 41*42*43 can be expressed as 41*6*7*43 or 6*(41*7*43). This shows that the product 41*42*43 is a multiple of 6.

So consider the case such as 43, 44, 45, where none of the three consecutive numbers is a multiple of 6. Dividing each of the three consecutive numbers by 6 will result in the remainders in the order 1-2-3, (43=6*7+1, 44=6*7+2, and 45=6*7+3.) Dividing each of **any** three consecutive numbers by 6 will result in one of three possible orderings of the remainders, either 1-2-3, or 2-3-4, or 3-4-5. For the case of 1-2-3 we have the form $(6J+1)(6J+2)(6J+3)=(6J+1)2(3J+1)3(2J+1)$ $=6(6J+1)(3J+1)(2J+1)$

For the case of 2-3-4 we have the form $(6J+2)(6J+3)(6J+4)=$ $2(3J+1)3(2J+1)(6J+4) =6(3J+1)(2J+1)(6J+4)$

For the case of 3-4-5 we have the form $(6J+3)(6J+4)(6J+5)$ $=3(2J+1)2(3J+2)(6J+5) =6(2J+1)(3J+2)(6J+5)$

Each of these three cases produces a factored form revealing that the product is always multiple of 6.

> "Defendit numerous: There is safety in numbers."
>
> —*Anonymous*

1.3 Isolating Digits in a Spreadsheet

Sometimes, as I am waking up, I realize that in my last moments of sleep, my mind has been considering some specific property of numbers that will suggest a possible area of exploration and discovery. As an illustration, consider a discovery that came to me as I reflected on the division-by-3 test discussed earlier. As I considered the powers of 3 (9, 27, 81, 243, 729, etc.) it occurred to me that, except for 3 itself, the sum of the digits of these numbers is always a multiple of 9.

A spreadsheet that computed and displayed the individual digits of a computed number would enable me to confirm my proposition. Before designing a spreadsheet, I explored the required computations with a calculator.

To compute and isolate the hundreds-digit, in a five-digit number such as X=54,632, I need to use the positional properties of this number. By this I mean to express 54,632 as 5*10000+4*1000+ 6*100+3*10+2. My goal is to isolate the 6, so I first divide 54,632 by both 100 and 1000 for the two numbers 546.32 and 54.632. The integer-value of these two numbers is 546 and 54, respectively. By multiplying 54 by 10 and subtracting the result from 546, I get 6, the hundreds-digit of the original 54,632. So the formula INT(54632/100)- 10*INT(54632/1000) will give me the 6.

I discovered that if X is number with at least three digits, then the formula INT(X/100)-10*INT(X/1000) will compute the hundreds-digit of X. In general, the Nth digit of a number X with at least N digits, can be computed with the spreadsheet formula, **$INT(X/10^{(N-1)})-10*INT(X/10^N)$**. Such formulas are used in a spreadsheet that computed the individual digits of powers of 3 as well as the sums of these digits. A chart from the spreadsheet is shown below. See **Appendix B** for the formulas used in this spreadsheet.

P	3^P	The digits of 3^P						Sum of the digits	
1	3	3							
2	9	9						=	9
3	27	2	7					=	9
4	81	8	1					=	9
5	243	2	4	3				=	9
6	729	7	2	9				=	18
7	2187	2	1	8	7		=		18
8	6561	6	5	6	1		=		18
9	19683	1	9	6	8	3		=	27
10	59049	5	9	0	4	9		=	27
11	177147	1	7	7	1	4	7	=	27
12	531441	5	3	1	4	4	1	=	18

The chart reveals that each sum computed is a multiple of 9. The evidence provided by the spreadsheet encouraged me to propose the theorem *"The sum of the digits of powers of 3 is a multiple of 9 when the power is greater than 2."*

The theorem is obviously true for 9, 27, and 81, the 2nd, 3rd, and 4th powers of 3. As an example of higher powers of 3 consider 3^9 = 19683=1*10000+9*1000+6*100+8*10+3.

Reformulate this to (1*9999+1)+(9*999+9)+(6*99+6)+(8*9+8)+3 and define S=1+9+6+8+3 the sum of the digits of 3^9, then we have 3^9=(1*9999)+(9*999)+(6*99)+(8*9)+S.

Therefore S=3^9-[(1*9999)+(9*999)+(6*99)+(8*9)].

From 3^9 = 9 * 3^7 we have S=9*3^7-9*[1111+9*111+6*11+8], a multiple of 9.

> "Nothing great in the World has been accomplished without passion."
> —*Georg Hegel*,
> German philosopher, 1832

1.4 Evens as Consecutive Sums

Several years ago, I was curious whether every even number could be expressed as the sum of consecutive numbers. I created a spreadsheet of consecutive sums of three numbers, four numbers, five numbers, seven numbers, and eight numbers. Consecutive sums of six numbers did not provide any new even numbers.

The chart below from the spreadsheet reveals sums of consecutive numbers for the even numbers 6 to 30, with the exception of 8 and 16. The asterisk following an even number indicates the first occurrence of the number. The chart shows 6=1+2+3, 10=1+2+3+4, 12=3+4+5, 14=2+3+4+5, 18=3+4+4+6, 20=2+3+4+5+6, 22=4+5+6+7, 24=7+8+9, 26=5+6+7+8, 28=1+2+3+4+5+6+7, and 30=4+5+6+7+8

	Sum of three	Sum of four	Sum of five	Sum of seven	Sum of eight
1					
2					
3	6*				
4	9	10*			
5	12*	14*	15		
6	15	18*	20*		
7	18	22*	25	28*	
8	21	26*	30*	35	36*

Providing consecutive sums for all even numbers from 6 to 100, with the exception of 8, 16, 32, and 64, required the numbers from 1 to 33 and consecutive sums of three, four, five, seven, eight, nine, and eleven numbers.

		Sum of three	Sum of four	Sum of five	Sum of seven	Sum of eight	Sum of nine	Sum of eleven
1								
2								
3		6*						
4		9	10*					
5		12*	14*	15				
6		15	18*	20*				
7		18	22*	25	28*			
8		21	26*	30*	35	36*		
9		24*	30	35	42*	44*	45	
10		27	34*	40*	49	52*	54*	
11		30	38*	45	56*	60*	63	66
12		33	42	50*	63	68*	72*	77
13		36	46*	55	70*	76*	81	88*
14		39	50	60	77	84*	90*	99
15		42	54	65	84	92*	99	110
16		45	58*	70	91	100*	108	121
17		48	62*	75	98*	108	117	132
18		51	66	80*	105	116	126	143
19		54	70	85	112	124	135	154
20		57	74*	90	119	132	144	165
21		60	78*	95	126	140	153	176
22		63	82*	100	133	148	162	187
23		66	86	105	140	156	171	198
24		69	90	110	147	164	180	209
25		72	94*	115	154	172	189	220
26		75	98	120	161	180	198	231
27		78	102*	125	168	188	207	242

28	81	106	130	175	196	216	253
29	84	110	135	182	204	225	264
30	87	114	140	189	212	234	275
31	90	118	145	196	220	243	286
32	93	122	150	203	228	252	297
33	96*	126	155	210	236	261	308

Encouraged by my spreadsheet, I proposed the proposition *"Every even number except powers of 2 can be expressed as a sum of consecutive numbers."*

I then created a *brute-force* search procedure to find the fewest consecutive numbers that would sum to an even number. Given an even number N, the sum will require at least three consecutive numbers, so the search starts with the series S=M+(M+1)+(M+2) where M equals to one more than the integer-value of N divided by 3.

For example if N=72, then M=24, so the initial sum S=24+25+26. The procedure then adds and subtracts numbers until the correct sum appears. Continuing the search for a series of consecutive numbers that sum to 72, we see that the initial sum 24+25+26=75 is too big. So subtract 26 and add 23, for 23+24+25, which is a series of consecutive numbers that sum to 72.

Some even numbers require considerable computation. For the even number N=58, S=19, and the initial series 19+20+21=60 is too big, so subtract 21 and add 18 for 18+19+20=57. This is too small, so add 17 for 17+18+19+20=74. This is too big, so subtract 20 and add 16 for 16+17+18+19=70. Subtract 19 and add 15 for 15+16+17+18=66. Subtract 18 and add 14 for 14+15+16+17=62 then subtract 17 and add 13 for 13+14+15+16=58. This is the series of consecutive numbers that sum to 58.

Computation consisting of lots of adding, subtracting, summing, and testing is more quickly performed by a computer, so I wrote a program that implemented my brute-force procedure. The output of the program convinced me that my conjecture was true. But neither a spreadsheet nor computer program constitutes a mathematical proof, leaving me with the need for a symbolic method.

My need was met the day after I presented my brute-force procedure to one of my high school classes. Student **Laura Adams** provided an elegant procedure for finding S, the smallest number that begins an appropriate consecutive sum. I call her procedure *Adams' Algorithm*.

Given an even number E other than a power of 2, let D be the largest odd divisor of E and let Q be the result of dividing E by D. Note that Q will always be a power of 2. Let L=(D-1)/2 and note that L is an even number because D is an odd number. If Q>L, let S=Q−L, otherwise let S=L−Q+1. The number S will be the leading number in the series that sums to the given even number E.

To clarify the procedure, consider the example where the even number E=56=8*7, then D=7, Q=8, and L=3. Since Q>L, use S=Q−L= 5, then 56=5+6+7+8+9+10+11.

For another example, consider the even number E=30=2*3*5, then D=15, Q=2, and L=7. Since Q<L, S=L-Q+1=6, then 30=6+7+8+9. See **Appendix C** for the design of a spreadsheet that implements **Adams' Algorithm**.

I was able to combine the two cases, Q>L and Q<L into one choice with S=Q-L. For the case where E=30, Q=2, and L=7, so Q<L. Now, using S=Q−L=-5, we have 30=[(-5-4-3-2-1+0)+(1+2+3+4+5]+[6+7+ 8+9] or 30=[-5+5-4+4-3+3-2+2-1+1+0]+[6+7+8+9]=6+7+8+9. In general, the required series of positive numbers results after adding the negative numbers to the corresponding positive numbers.

Note that for the number 72, **Adams' Algorithm** gives S=4, so 72=4+5+6+7+8+9+10+11+12, while my brute-force method gives 72=23+24+25. I prefer my method, but could not design a corresponding spreadsheet.

Adams' Algorithm took care of all but the exclusion of powers of 2. A colleague, **Marshal Ransom**, was able to prove indirectly *"No power of 2 is expressible as a sum of consecutive numbers."* We now have the **Adams-Ransom Theorem**: *"Every even number except powers of 2* can be expressed as a sum of consecutive numbers."

> "Mathematics, rightly viewed, possesses not only truth, but supreme beauty – a beauty cold and austere, like that of sculpture."
> —Bertrand Russell

1.5 Expanding the Concept of Number

The Pythagoreans thought that the natural numbers such as 1, 2, 3, 4, 5, etc. and the ratios of these numbers were sufficient for all measurements of lengths. Consider a square with sides of length 1. Two adjacent sides and a connected diagonal of this square form a right triangle. Let D represent the length of the diagonal, then by the **Pythagorean Theorem**, $D^2=1^2+1^2=2$. The next theorem is significant because it reveals that there is no number D such that $D^2=2$.

Theorem C: "*It is impossible to find two whole numbers such that the square of one of them is equal to twice the square of the other (i.e. $J^2 \neq 2K^2$ for any whole numbers J and K).*"

Proof: Suppose, to the contrary, we have numbers N and M, where $N^2=2M^2$. By repeatedly dividing both sides of this equation by 2, we can assume that both N and M are not simultaneously even. From $N^2=2M^2$, N^2 is even, so from **Theorem B**, N must be even. Since there is a quotient Q such that N=2Q, the equation $N^2=2M^2$ becomes $4Q^2=2M^2$ which reduces to $2Q^2=M^2$, revealing that M^2 is even and hence again by **Theorem B**, M is even. But N and M cannot both be even because we factored out all the common 2's. We therefore have a contradiction to the fact that equations can be simplified by factoring and dividing.

The Pythagorean Theorem, together with **Theorem B** and **Theorem C**, reveal that mathematicians needed to expand the set of numbers that the Pythagoreans thought sufficient for measurements. The diagonal of any square that has sides of natural number length will have non-rational measures. We call these measures *irrational numbers* and they include the square-roots of numbers that are not perfect squares $\sqrt{2}$, $\sqrt{3}$, $\sqrt{5}$, $\sqrt{7}$, etc.

> *"A proof tells us where to concentrate our doubts."*
>
> —*Morris Kline*

1.6 Mathematical Induction

The proofs of **Theorem C** and **Ransom's Theorem** both began with the phrase "*Suppose to the contrary....*" This type of proof is called an *indirect proof* or *a proof by contradiction*. Mathematicians turn to this method when a direct method fails to yield success. Later we will learn that Euclid used an indirect proof to demonstrate that there is no largest prime number. Mathematicians have another method to use when they are trying to establish that all members of an infinite set have some specified property. It is called *mathematical induction* and is justified by the statement *"Any non-empty subset of natural numbers contains a smallest number,"* a self-evident statement that is the result of one of the nine axioms of arithmetic. See **Appendix G** for all nine axioms and a discussion of arithmetic as an axiomatic theory.

To establish that all numbers in an infinite collection S have a specified property P, proof by induction has only two requirements. First, one must establish that the smallest number in S satisfies the property P; and secondly, one must establish that if N satisfies property P, then the next number, N+1 also satisfies property P.

It is easy to discover that no matter how many odd numbers you use, if you start with the number one and add the next umpteen odd numbers, you will get a square number. For example, $1+3+5+7+9+11=36=6^2$. I will use $2N-1$ to represent the Nth odd number and mathematical induction to prove *"The sum of N consecutive odd numbers, beginning* *with the number 1, equals N^2"*

Proof: Let S represent the collection of all numbers N having the property, $1+3+5+...+(2N-1)=N^2$. S contains 1, 2, and 3 because $1=1^2$, $1+3=4=2^2$, and $1+3+5=9=3^2$. We now need only show that if S contains the number N, then S will also contain the next number, N+1.

If S contains N, then $1+3+5+...+(2N-1)=N^2$. Now add the next odd number $(2N+1)$ to both sides of the above equation for the equation for $1+3+5+...+(2N-1)+(2N+1)=N^2+(2N+1)$.

The expression N^2+2N+1 equals $(N+1)^2$, therefore $1+3+5+...+(2N-1)+(2N+1)=(N+1)^2$, establishing that S contains N+1.

For an interesting extension of the above theorem, notice that $2^2-1=3$ and $3+5=8=2^3$ and that $3^2-2=7$ while $7+9+11=27=3^3$.

Continuing in a similar manner $4^2-3=13$ while $13+15+17+19=64=4^3$ and $5^2-4=21$ while $21+22+23+24+25=125=5^3$. In general N^3 will equal the sum of N consecutive odd numbers beginning with the number $N^2-(N-1)$.

To prove this first note that $N^2-(N-1)=N^2-N+1$. Secondly $N^2-(N-1)$ is an odd number because if on the one hand N is even then N^2 is even and N-1 is odd, thus their difference is odd. On the other hand if N is odd then N^2 is odd and N-1 is even so again their difference is odd.

Starting with N^2-N+1 and summing the next N odd numbers results in $(N^2-N+1)+(N^2-N+3)+(N^2-N+5)+...$ where the last term is $[(N^2-N+(2N-1))]$. Since each of the N terms contains the expression N^2-N the sum can be re-expressed as $(N^2-N)*N+[1+3+5+...(2N-1)]$ or $(N^2-N)*N+N^2=N^3-N^2+N^2=N^3$

Only a few of the propositions of this chapter are significant. They were presented to give the reader a sense of how representing expressions can lead to a mathematical proof. The propositions and proofs treated in the next chapter came to us from earlier times. Three of them provide evidence that Euclid was a mathematical genius.

> "An intelligent observer seeing mathematicians at work might conclude that they are devotees of exotic sects, pursuers of esoteric keys to the universe."
> –**Philip Davis** and **Reuben Hersh**,
> The Mathematical Experience

CHAPTER TWO
Numbers: Friendly, Perfect, and Prime

2.1 Mutually Friendly Numbers

There are few written records from antiquity regarding Pythagoras. He lived sometime between 580 and 500 BC and is mostly a legend. Our knowledge of his mathematics was conveyed by those who came after him. Legend has it that Pythagoras believed that numbers held mystical and religious powers. He reportedly formed a group of followers who believed about numbers as he did. The statement "All is number" is attributed to him, but to attribute something to Pythagoras is to attribute it to the Pythagoreans, the members of his school or cult.

The Pythagoreans believed that numbers were godly and deserved respect. For example, 2 is the smallest female number and 3 the smallest male number, so 5, the sum of 2 and 3 stood for marriage. The moon, sun, and the planets formed seven heavenly objects, so the number 7 was awesome. The number 10 is the sum of 1 (the dimensions of a point), 2 (the number of points needed for a line), 3 (the number of points needed for a triangle), and 4 (the number of points needed to describe space).

The Pythagoreans defined two numbers to be *friends* if the proper

Numbers: Friendly, Perfect, and Prime

divisors of one summed to the other, and vice versa. The *proper divisors* of a number N are the numbers that will divide N evenly with the exception of the number N itself. For example the numbers 1, 2, 3, and 6 will divide 6 evenly, but only 1, 2, and 3 are proper divisors of 6.

The smallest pair of numbers that are friends are 220 and 284. The sum of the proper divisors of 284 (1+2+4+71+142) equals 220 and the sum of the proper divisors of 220 (1+2+4+5+10+11+20+22+44+55+110) equals 284.

For centuries, no other pair of friendly numbers was found, until in 1636, Fermat discovered that the numbers 17,296 and 18,416 are friends. In 1866, a young Italian boy, whose name has been forgotten, discovered that the numbers 1,184 and 1,210 are friends.

See **Appendix D** for an explanation of a spreadsheet created to confirm that 1184 and 1210 are friends.

	2	4	8	16	17	18	19	20	21	32	***1184***
	592	296	148	74	69.7	65.8	62.3	59.2	56	37	
	1	1	1	1	0	0	0	0	0	1	
1	594	300	156	90	0	0	0	0	0	69	***1210***
	2	5	10	11	12	13	14	15	16	22	***1210***
	605	242	121	110	101	93.1	86.4	80.7	76	55	
	1	1	1	1	0	0	0	0	0	1	
1	607	247	131	121	0	0	0	0	0	77	***1184***

> *"The prime numbers... grow like weeds among the natural numbers, seeming to obey no other law than that of chance, and nobody can predict where the next one will sprout."*
>
> —*Don Zagier*

2.2 Prime Numbers

Pythagoras, Euclid, and Fermat were each interested in prime numbers. By definition, a number is a *prime number* if it has exactly two divisors, the numbers 1 and the number itself. A prime number P is a multiple of only P. The definition is stated so that the number 1 is not a prime number. These numbers are the building blocks of arithmetic, providing for all numbers as the elements of the periodic table provide for chemical compounds.

Using prime numbers and multiplication, there is essentially only one way to express the number 72, namely 72=2*2*2*3*3. The expression 2*2*2*3*3 is called the prime-decomposition of 72. The prime decomposition of each number is unique, a fact so important that it is called **The Fundamental Theorem of Arithmetic**. The first seven prime numbers are 2, 3, 5, 7, 11, 13, and 17. We will soon learn that the collection is unlimited.

A spreadsheet uses the first six odd prime numbers to find the next twelve prime numbers. In the related chart below, the numbers in the first column (19, 21, 23, etc.) are divided in turn by the prime numbers (3, 5, 7, etc.) in the first row to produce the corresponding remainders in columns two thru six. A row containing 0 indicates that the number in the first column is a composite number and therefore not a prime number.

	3	5	7	11	13	17	
19	1	4	5	8	6	2	Prime
21	0	1	0	10	8	4	
23	2	3	2	1	10	6	Prime
25	1	0	4	3	12	8	
27	0	2	6	5	1	10	
29	2	4	1	7	3	12	Prime
31	1	1	3	9	5	14	Prime
33	0	3	5	0	7	16	

35	2	0	0	2	9	1	
37	1	2	2	4	11	3	Prime
39	0	4	4	6	0	5	
41	2	1	6	8	2	7	Prime
43	1	3	1	10	4	9	Prime
45	0	0	3	1	6	11	
47	2	2	5	3	8	13	Prime
49	1	4	0	5	10	15	
51	0	1	2	7	12	0	
53	2	3	4	9	1	2	Prime
55	1	0	6	0	3	4	
57	0	2	1	2	5	6	
59	2	4	3	4	7	8	Prime
61	1	1	5	6	9	10	Prime
63	0	3	0	8	11	12	
65	2	0	2	10	0	14	
67	1	2	4	1	2	16	Prime

The Greek mathematician, Eratosthenes, devised a method for generating a list of the first few prime numbers. Eratosthenes had to use a primitive writing method to demonstrate his method, but I am able to use a spreadsheet to illustrate his procedure to find the prime numbers less than 100.

The sieve starts with a list of consecutive numbers beginning with the number 2.

	2	3	4	5	6	7	8	9	10
11	12	13	14	15	16	17	18	19	20
21	22	23	24	25	26	27	28	29	30
31	32	33	34	35	36	37	38	39	40
41	42	43	44	45	46	47	48	49	50
51	52	53	54	55	56	57	58	59	60
61	62	63	64	65	66	67	68	69	70

71	72	73	74	75	76	77	78	79	80
81	82	83	84	85	86	87	88	89	90
92	92	93	94	95	96	97	98	99	100

Then 4 and all multiples of 2 are eliminated.

	2	3	5	7	9
11		13	15	17	19
21		23	25	27	29
31		33	35	37	39
41		43	45	47	49
51		53	55	57	59
61		63	65	67	69
71		73	75	77	79
81		83	85	87	89
91		93	95	97	99

Then 9 and all multiples of 3 are eliminated.

	2	3	5	7	
11		13		17	19
		23	25		29
31			35	37	
41		43		47	49
		53	55		59
61			65	67	
71		73		77	79
		83	85		89
91			95	97	

Then 25 and all multiples of 5 are eliminated.

	2	3	5	7	
11		13		17	19
		23			29
31				37	
41		43		47	49
		53			59
61				67	
71		73		77	79
		83			89
91				97	

Then 49 and all multiples of 7 are eliminated.

	2	3	5	7	
11		13		17	19
		23	25		29
31			35	37	
41		43		47	49
		53	55		59
61			65	67	
71		73		77	79
		83	85		89
91			95	97	

The twenty-five numbers that remain are prime numbers.

To study some properties of prime numbers, I wrote a computer program that found the first ten thousand prime numbers, and stored them in a file on my computer. The program used subtraction to determine the remainder when a candidate X is divided by the prime number 3 (X=3*Q+R). If the remainder was zero, then X was a composite number. If the remainder was not zero, then the test continues by expressing X in terms of P the next prime numbers (X=P*Q+R). The process ended when either the remainder was zero or when the quotient Q was less than the prime-divisor P. A zero remainder meant that X was a composite number.

I will illustrate the computer process by finding the next prime number after 97. The next candidate must be an odd number, so 99 is tested. Subtracting the prime number 3 from 99 thirty-three times leaves the remainder 0 (99=3*33+0) therefore 99 is not a prime number. Next, the number 101 is tested. Subtracting 3 from 101 thirty-three times results in the remainder 1 (101=3*33+1). Subtracting 5, the next prime number from 101 twenty times results in the remainder 1 (101=5*20+1). Subtracting 7, the next prime number from 101 fourteen times results in the remainder 3 (101=7*14+3). Subtracting 11, the next prime number from 101 nine times results in the remainder 2 (101=11*9+2). Note that the quotient 9 is less than the prime divisor 11.

There is no need to express 101 in terms of prime numbers larger than 11, because the corresponding quotients will all be smaller than the dividing prime number. Therefore the next prime number after 97 is 101.

To help clarify the prime divisors that are sufficient for testing a candidate number X, consider the testing of X=283. If we express 283 in terms of small primes and the corresponding decimal quotients, we have 3*94.333, 5*56.6, 7*40.429, 11*25.727, 13*21.769, 17*16.647, 19*14.895, 23*12.304, etc. Notice that divisors and quotients come in pairs and a prime divisor larger than 17, which is a bit larger than the square root of 283 (approximately 16.8227) results in a quotient smaller than the divisor. The point is, when testing a candidate X for primality, there is no need to test with primes larger than the square root of X.

Below is a list of the first 104 prime numbers generated by the program.

2	43	103	173	241	317	401	479
3	47	107	179	251	331	409	487
5	53	109	181	257	337	419	491
7	59	113	191	263	347	421	499
11	61	127	193	269	349	431	503
13	67	131	197	271	353	433	509
17	71	137	199	277	359	439	521
19	73	139	211	281	367	443	523
23	79	149	223	283	373	449	541
29	83	151	227	293	379	457	547
31	89	157	229	307	383	461	557
37	97	163	233	311	389	463	563
41	101	167	239	313	397	467	569

"The different branches of Arithmetic: Ambition, Distraction, Uglification, and Derision."

—*Lewis Carroll*

2.3 Decomposing a Composite Number

High school students are asked to decompose small numbers into a product of prime numbers. They use their results to simplify radicals. For example:

$$\sqrt{72}\sqrt{2\cdot2\cdot2\cdot3\cdot3}\quad 2\cdot3\sqrt{2}\quad \sqrt{2}$$
$$\sqrt{72}\sqrt{2\cdot2\cdot2\cdot3\cdot3}\sqrt{2\cdot2\cdot2}\sqrt{3\cdot3}\quad 2\sqrt{}$$

I wrote a computer program that used my file of prime numbers to calculate the prime divisors of a number and display it in prime-decomposition form. In their search for large prime numbers, early mathematicians had proposed that some specific numbers were probably prime numbers. The program enabled me to test some of these numbers to determine if they are prime numbers. The four decompositions shown below indicate that these numbers are not prime numbers.

$2^{11}-1=2047=23*89$
$2^{23}-1=8388607=47*178481$
$2^{29}-536870911=233*1103*2089$
$2^{37}-1=137438953471=223*616318177$

> *"I have no special talents. I am only passionately curious."*
> —Albert Einstein

2.4 Euclid's Search for Prime Numbers

Euclid is most famous for his work regarding geometry. He began the idea of treating a mathematical theory as the result of axioms, a few self-evident statements, from which other propositions would logically follow. He left us his "*Elements*," thirteen books that start with five axioms that define plane geometry, then continue with definitions and proofs of many geometric propositions. Euclid's axiomatic approach to geometry is studied today by students all over the world.

Euclid was also interested in numbers. In *Elements*, Euclid briefly treated arithmetic and proved some theorems regarding numbers. Like Pythagoras before him, Euclid was interested in prime numbers and discovered a method for finding prime numbers larger than any in a collection of given prime numbers. He noticed that adding the number 1 to the product of the first few prime numbers would reveal prime numbers larger than any used in the product. For example

2*3*5*7+1=211, a prime number larger than the prime numbers 2, 3, 5, or 7. The chart below will further illustrate the idea.

PRIMES NUMBERS	PRODUCTS OF PRIMES	PRODUCTS PLUS 1	PRIME FACTORS		
2	2				
3	6	7	NONE		
5	30	31	NONE		
7	210	211	NONE		
11	2310	2311	NONE		
13	30030	30031	509		
17	510510	510511	19	97	277
19	9699690	9699691	347	27953	
23	223092870	223092871	317	703763	
29	6469693230	6469693231	331	571	34231

Notice that using the ten smallest prime numbers renders eleven more, each larger than any of the original ten.

From his discovery, Euclid realized that there could not be a largest prime number, and used the method of his discovery to prove "*There is no largest prime number.*" His proof is indirect and begins with a supposition that leads to a contradiction. Euclid supposes to the contrary that there is a largest prime number P. He then defines a number Q as 1 plus the product of all the prime number from 2 to P. He uses the number Q to derive a contradiction to arithmetic which results in the conclusion that there must be a prime number larger than P. Perhaps an example will help you follow his reasoning. Suppose, for example, one believes that 29 is the largest prime number. Euclid's number Q will be equal to 2*3*5*7*11*13*17*19*23*29 +1 which equals 6469693231. Euclid then argues that because this number Q is larger than 29 it must be a multiple of one of the prime numbers used to define it.

Euclid then selects one of the prime numbers that is supposedly a multiple of Q. For example, if Euclid selects the prime number 13, then Q=13J for some number J.

Defining $L = Q-1 = 2*3*5*7*11*13*17*19*23*29$ results in the equation $1 = Q-L$. Substituting 13J for Q in the equation $1 = Q-L$ results in the equation $1 = 13J - 2*3*5*7*11*13*17*19*23*29$.

Factoring the 13 on the right side results in the equation $1 = 13(J - 2*3*5*7*11*17*19*23*29)$. This equation implies that the number 1 is a multiple of the number 13, a contradiction to arithmetic.

If Euclid had selected any of the prime divisors of Q and expressed Q as a multiple of that selection, the implication would again lead to a similar contradiction. See **Appendix F** for a more formal demonstration of Euclid's theorem.

> "A formal manipulator in mathematics often experiences the discomforting feeling that his pencil surpasses him in intelligence."
> —*Howard W. Eves*

2.5 Euclid's Algorithm

With his interest in numbers, Euclid needed to calculate the largest number G that would divide evenly into two given numbers, M and N. This number G is called the greatest common divisor, or GCD of M and N. It is easy to see that 1 is the GCD of 5 and 7 and that 5 is the GCD of 35 and 55, but Euclid needed to find the GCD of two large numbers. I will illustrate Euclid's algorithm by finding the GCD of 3640 and 3757.

Begin by finding the quotient and remainder when 3757 is divided by 3640, $3757 = 1*3640 + 117$. Next find the quotient and remainder when 3640 is divided by 117, $3640 = 31*117 + 13$. Now find the quotient and remainder when 117 is divided by 13, $117 = 9*13 + 0$. The last non-zero remainder was 13, so 13 is the GCD of 3640 and 3757 ($3640 = 13*280$ and $3757 = 13*289$). Note that since $280 = 2*2*2*3*5*7$ and $289 = 17*17$, these two numbers have no common divisors.

To perform Euclid's algorithm to find the GCD of M and N, divide N by M and express N in terms of the divisor M, the quotient Q1, and the remainder R1 (N=Q1*M+R1). Then express M in terms of the divisor R1, a new quotient Q2, and a new remainder R2 (M=Q2*R1+R2). Continue dividing the previous remainder by the new remainder and express the previous remainder in terms of the new quotient and the new remainder until the new remainder is 0. The GCD of M and N will be the last non-zero remainder.

Euclid's algorithm is used below to calculate the greatest common divisor of 11557 and 16471.

16471=1*11557+4914
11557=2*4914+1729
4914=2*1729+1456
1729=1*1456+273
1456=5*273+91
273=3*91+0

So 91=7*13 is the GCD of 11557 and 16471 as confirmed by the prime decompositions, 11557=7*13*127 and 16471 =7*13*181.

> *"You can only find truth with logic if you have already found truth without it."*
> —G.K. Chesterton

2.6 Euclid's Search for Perfect Numbers

Some three hundred years before Euclid, Pythagoras, with his mystical and religious view of numbers, defined a number to be *perfect* if it equals to the sum of its proper divisors. The number 6 equals the sum of 1, 2, 3, and 1, 2, and 3 are the proper divisors of 6. For Pythagoras, God took six days to create the universe because 6 is a perfect number.

The number of days between one full moon and the next is 28 because 28 is a perfect number. The proper divisors of 28 are 1, 2, 4, 7, and 14, and 28=1+2+4+7+14.

Euclid was also interested in *perfect* numbers and studied the powers of 2 as a possible source of perfect numbers. He considered powers of 2 because they each have only one prime divisor, and thus have limited and easily found proper divisors. For example the proper divisors of $8=2^3$ are $1=2^0, 2=2^1$, and $4=2^2$. In general the proper divisors of 2^N are 2^P, where P has values 0 to N-1.

See **Appendix E** for a spreadsheet that calculates the sum of the proper divisors of small powers of 2. A related chart reveals that the sums equal to one less than the power, $1+2+2^2+\ldots+2^{N-2}+2^{N-1}=2^N-1$.

	2	4	8	16	32	64	128	256	512	1024	2048	
16	1	1	1	1	0	0	0	0	0	0	0	
	1	1	1	0	1	1	1	1	1	1	1	SUM
1	2	4	8	0	0	0	0	0	0	0	0	15
32	2	4	8	16	32	64	128	256	512	1024	2048	
	1	1	1	1	1	0	0	0	0	0	0	
	1	1	1	1	0	1	1	1	1	1	1	SUM
1	2	4	8	16	0	0	0	0	0	0	0	31
64	2	4	8	16	32	64	128	256	512	1024	2048	
	1	1	1	1	1	1	0	0	0	0	0	
	1	1	1	1	1	0	1	1	1	1	1	SUM
1	2	4	8	16	32	0	0	0	0	0	0	63
128	2	4	8	16	32	64	128	256	512	1024	2048	
	1	1	1	1	1	1	1	0	0	0	0	
	1	1	1	1	1	1	0	1	1	1	1	SUM
1	2	4	8	16	32	64	0	0	0	0	0	127
256	2	4	8	16	32	64	128	256	512	1024	2048	
	1	1	1	1	1	1	1	1	0	0	0	
	1	1	1	1	1	1	1	0	1	1	1	SUM
1	2	4	8	16	32	64	128	0	0	0	0	255
512	2	4	8	16	32	64	128	256	512	1024	2048	

	1	1	1	1	1	1	1	1	1	0	0	
	1	1	1	1	1	1	1	1	0	1	1	SUM
1	2	4	8	16	32	64	128	256	0	0	0	511

Theorem E: *"For each number N, the sum of the proper divisors of 2^N equals 2^N-1.*

Proof by induction:

Let S be the collection of the numbers N that satisfy the equation $1+2+2^2+2^3+\ldots+2^{N-2}+2^{N-1}=2^N-1$

S contains 1, 2, and 3, because $1=2^1-1=2^0$, $1+2=3=2^2-1$, and $1+2+2^2=7=2^3-1$.

Induction requires us to demonstrate that if S contains N then S must also contain N+1. By assumption S contains N, so $1+2+2^2+\ldots+2^{N-2}+2^{N-1}=2^N-1$ Adding 2^N to both sides of this equations results in the equation, $1+2+2^2+2^3+\ldots+2^{N-2}+2^{N-1}+2^N=2^N-1+2^N$.

Since $2^N-1+2^N=2*2^N-1=2^{(N+1)}-1$, S also contains N+1. Euclid must have also considered the sum of the divisors of numbers like $5*2^N$ and $13*2^N$, i.e. products of odd prime number and powers of 2 and discovered that these sums are very similar to the sums he already had. For example, the proper divisors of $7*2^5$ are 1, 2, 2^2, 2^3, 2^4, 2^5 as well as $7*1, 7*2, 7*2^2, 7*2^3, 7*2^4$.

Observations similar to the ones above probably led Euclid to what I consider to be his most beautiful theorem: *"If 2^P-1 is a prime number, then $(2^P-1)*2^{(P-1)}$ is a perfect number."*

Euclid knew of only four perfect numbers, yet his theorem promised that there are more, if only future mathematicians can find some prime numbers of a specific form. I will use an example to illustrate how the theorem is proved.

The prime number $31=(2^5-1)$ and $2^{(5-1)}=2^4=16$, so let $S=(2^5-1)*2^{(5-1)}=31*16=496$ which has proper divisors 1, 2, 2^2, 2^3, 2^4 and $31*1, 31*2, 31*2^2, 31*2^3$.

Let T represent the sum of these proper divisors of S then $T=(1+2+2^2+2^3)+2^4+(2^5-1)(1+2+2^2+2^3)$.

From **Theorem E**, $(1+2+2^2+2^3)=2^4-1$ so $T=(2^4-1)+2^4+(2^5-1)*(2^4-1)$

or $T=(2^4+2^4-1)+(2^5-1)*(2^4-1)$.

Therefore $T=(2*2^4-1)+(2^5-1)*(2^4-1)$ or
$T=(2^5-1)+(2^5-1)(2^4-1)=(2^5-1)*(1+(2^4-1))$. So $T=(2^5-1)*2^4$ or $(2^5-1)*2^{(5-1)}$ which equals S. Since 496 equals the sum of its proper divisors, it is a perfect number.

A spreadsheet was able to confirm that some numbers are perfect. The sheet calculated the sum of the proper divisors of the number in the top right and displays the sum in the bottom right.

	2	3	4	5	8	10	16	32	37	496
	248	165.33	124	99.2	62	49.6	31	15.5	13.41	
	1	0	1	0	1	0	1	0	0	
1	250	0	128	0	70	0	47	0	0	496

	2	3	4	5	8	10	16	32	64	8128
	4064	2709.3	2032	1625.6	1016	812.8	508	254	127	
	1	0	1	0	1	0	1	1	1	
1	4066	0	2036	0	1024	0	524	286	191	8128

This brings us to the question "Are there any other perfect numbers?" Euclid's theorem implies that there are others, provided there are more prime number of the form 2^P-1.

The fifth perfect number was found centuries after Euclid when it was discovered that $2^{13}-1$ is a prime number. The fifth perfect number is $(2^{13}-1)*2^{12}=33550336$, so it should not surprise us that Euclid never found this rather large number.

Any perfect number that is the result of Euclid's theorem is an even number. No one has ever found an odd perfect number, and mathematicians have yet to prove that there are none. In the next chapter, we will encounter more large numbers and learn if Fermat had anything to add to this search for perfect numbers.

> *"To Thales . . . the primary question was not what do we know but how do we know it."*
> —**Aristotle**

Chapter Three
A Passion for Large Numbers

3.1 Fermat's Infinite Descent

Pierre de Fermat (1601 – 1665), like Pythagoras and Euclid, became enchanted with the hidden properties of numbers. Although Fermat was a lawyer by profession, his fame is due to his work as an amateur mathematician. He somehow found time to contribute to various areas of mathematics, including differential calculus and probability. But his greatest contributions to mathematics were his discoveries regarding numbers.

Fermat discovered an interesting fact about prime numbers. He reasoned that there were two types of prime numbers: those that leave a remainder of 3 when divided by 4 and those that leave a remainder of 1 when divided by 4. For the prime numbers in this latter group, he proved that each could be expressed as the sum of two square numbers. For example dividing the prime number 53 by 4 leaves 1 as remainder (53=4*13+1) and a search reveals that 53=4+49 (2^2+7^2). In like manner the prime number 373 equals 4*93+1 and a search reveals that 373=49+324 (7^2+18^2).

To prove his theorem *"Every prime number of the form 4J+1 can be expressed as the sum of two square numbers,"* Fermat created an entirely new method to demonstrate its truth.

The method is called *infinite-descent* and I will use the method to prove the much simpler proposition "$\sqrt{3}$ *cannot be expressed as the ratio of two numbers.*"

For his proof of *"Every prime number of the form 4J+1 can be expressed as the sum of two square numbers,"* Fermat used an indirect argument by supposing to the contrary that there is a prime number of the form 4J+1 which is **not** the sum of two squares. He then showed that this supposition would lead to the existence of a smaller prime of the form 4J+1 which is also **not** the sum of two squares, therefore beginning a descent. Each smaller prime number of the form 4J+1 and **not** the sum of two squares, led to an even smaller prime number of the form 2J+1 and **not** the sum of two squares. The descent is necessarily finite and ends at the prime number 5. But 5 is both of the form 4J+1 (5=4*1+1) and the sum of two squares (5=1^2+2^2).

Fermat arrived at a contradiction and thus the original supposition was false.

> *"To divide a cube into two other cubes, a fourth power or in general any power whatever into two powers of the same denomination above the second is impossible, and I have assuredly found an admirable proof of this, but the margin is too narrow to contain it."*
> —*Pierre De Fermat*

3.2 Fermat's Last Theorem

Fermat's interest in specific properties of numbers was prompted by a math book he often studied. The book was a Latin translation of *Arithmetica*, a text which originated with Diophantus, a Greek algebraist who lived in Alexandria in the second century AD. The book explores some 150 problems, each with a solution that is a natural number.

Fermat became very interested in equations that have solutions that are natural numbers.

The equation $a^2+b^2=c^2$ from the theorem of Pythagoras provides lots of examples of such equations. The equation $a^2+4^2=5^2$ has a=3 as its only solution. The equation $a^2+b^2=25^2$ has a=7 and b=24 as its only solution.

An unlimited quantity of Pythagorean triples can be found that are natural number solutions to the Pythagorean equation $a^2+b^2=c^2$. One way to generates these triples is to substitute two natural numbers X and Y, where X>Y, into the formulas $a=X^2-Y^2$, $b=2XY$, and $c=X^2+Y^2$. For example, substituting X=4 and Y=9, gives a=65, b=72, and c=97, where, $65^2+72^2=4225+5184=9409=97^2$.

When the triple is primitive, (i.e. when a, b, and c have no common divisor) the process is reversible. For example, given the Pythagorean triple a=5, b=12, and c=13, the equations $7=X^2-Y^2$, $24=2XY$, and $25=X^2+Y^2$, when algebraically manipulated lead to $(X^2-Y^2)+(X^2+Y^2)=7+25=32=2X^2$. This leads to $X^2=16$, and hence X = 4. With X=4 and 24=2XY, 24=8Y, thus Y = 3.

The numbers in the triple 14-48-50 have 2 as a common divisor. If we attempt to discover the numbers X and Y that produce the triad as we did above, we will have $14=X^2-Y^2$, $48=2XY$, and $50=X^2+Y^2$, then $(X^2-Y^2)+(X^2+Y^2)=2X^2=14+50=64$, so $X^2=32$, which is not a perfect square. So the reversal process does not work for non-primitive triples.

The next spreadsheet uses the formulas, $A=X^2-Y^2$, $B=2XY$ and $C=X^2+Y^2$ to produce 54 Pythagorean triples.

X	Y	A	B	C	XY	A	B	C
1	2	3	4	5	1	12 | 143	24	145
2	3	5	12	13	5	12 | 119	120	169
1	4	15	8	17	7	12 | 95	168	193
3	4	7	24	25	2	13 | 165	52	173
2	5	21	20	29	4	13 | 153	104	185
4	5	9	40	41	6	13 | 133	156	205

1	6	35	12	37	8	13	105	208	233
5	6	11	60	61	10	13	69	260	269
2	7	45	28	53	12	13	25	312	313
4	7	33	56	65	1	14	195	28	197
6	7	13	84	85	3	14	187	84	205
1	8	63	16	65	5	14	171	140	221
3	8	55	48	73	9	14	115	252	277
5	8	39	80	89	11	14	75	308	317
7	8	15	112	113	13	14	27	364	365
2	9	77	36	85	2	15	221	60	229
4	9	65	72	97	4	15	209	120	241
8	9	17	144	145	8	15	161	240	289
1	10	99	20	101	14	15	29	420	421
3	10	91	60	109	1	16	255	32	257
5	10	75	100	125	3	16	247	96	265
7	10	51	140	149	5	16	231	160	281
9	10	19	180	181	7	16	207	224	305
2	11	117	44	125	9	16	175	288	337
4	11	105	88	137	11	16	135	352	377
6	11	85	132	157	13	16	87	416	425
8	11	57	176	185	15	16	31	480	481

Fermat used the reversible process of primitive triples and his method of infinite-descent to prove *"The equation $a^4+b^4=c^2$ has no solutions."* As a corollary to this theorem, the equation $a^4+b^4=c^4$ has no solution, for if it did then the equation $a^4+b^4=(c^2)^2$ would have a solution, contrary to the theorem.

Fermat then made a very bold conjecture, stating, *"For every natural number N greater than 2, equations of the form $a^N+b^N=c^N$, have no solutions."* He even claimed to have envisioned a proof, writing in the margin of his copy of *Arithmetica*, *"… and I have assuredly found an admirable proof of this, but the margin is too narrow to contain it."*

Fermat died in 1665, leaving behind a mystery that took some 350 years to solve. He had earned a great reputation that inspired many mathematicians to try their hand at resolving the puzzle. A list of mathematicians who worked on this elusive puzzle includes many who are famous for other achievements. In order of their birth, the list includes Leonhard Euler (1707), Sophie Germain (1776), Carl Friedrich Gauss (1777), Augustin-Louis Cauchy (1789), and Ernst Eduard Kummer (1810). The amateur mathematician Paul Wolfskehl (1856-1906) worked on the problem, failed, and then put up some prize money to be collected by whoever was first to solve the mystery.

By the year 1985, all but one of Fermat's discoveries and conjectures had been resolved, one way or the other, and most had been proven correct. But Fermat's theorem *"For every natural number N greater than 2, equations of the form $a^N+b^N=c^N$, have no solution"* remained unresolved. It came to be called *Fermat's Last Theorem* and remained only a conjecture for more than 350 years.

By the nineteenth and late twentieth century, mathematicians had developed powerful techniques for solving problems results that helped produce partial solutions to Fermat's conjecture.

Most mathematicians became convinced that Fermat had not actually discovered "*… an admirable proof of this ….*" But Fermat's reputation was such that they suspected that the conjecture was true. In fact, by 1985 the conjecture had been proven true for all numbers N up to four million.

But even that large number was insufficient for the British mathematician Andrew Wiles, who had heard about the unsolved problem when he was only ten. Even at that young age, Wiles dreamed of some day finding a solution or proof. With a deep passion for mathematics, Wiles began his serious search relatively late in his career. His encouragement came upon learning that the solution of another math problem of which he had deep knowledge would imply the universal truth of Fermat's Last Theorem.

So beginning in 1986, Wiles spent the next seven years working alone, studying the results of mathematicians who had previously worked on the problem. He was determined to find a proof of this elusive problem. He worked every day on this one mathematics problem, seldom leaving his house for anything but mundane tasks.

In the spring of 1993, Wiles had what he thought was a logical proof, and presented his results at an international math conference. He immediately became famous and was sought after by the news media for interviews. A month or so after his presentation, another mathematician found a logical gap in the purported proof. Wiles recognized his oversight and publically admitted the need for further work on the proof.

Wiles was determined to fill this logical gap and teamed up with the mathematician who had discovered the error. He used this mathematician as a sounding board for any new results he found. It took Wiles another year, but in the end he had a proof that met the rigorous judgment of other mathematicians. He had achieved that which had eluded so many before. He had earned fame and the prize money established by Wolfskehl. But more importantly, he followed his passion and had established his legacy as a great mathematician.

> *"The search for truth is more precious than its possession."*
> —*Albert Einstein*

3.3 Fermat's Search for a Formula

Fermat was aware of an ancient Chinese conjecture stating *"If a number N divides (2^N-2) then N is a prime number."* He found a counter example with N=341. Fermat discovered that 341 divides 2^{341}-2, but not a prime number because 341=11*31. I find this to be surprising because the program *Mathematica* calculates 2^{341}-2 equal to 4479489 4843556084211148845611368885562432909944692990697999 7820192758374236032189076175498654321 4231550, a number that is a whooping 103 digits long. Did Fermat actually calculate this number? How was Fermat able to decide that it is divisible by 341?

His counter-example led Fermat to his second famous theorem: *"If P is a prime number then for every number N, P divides N^P-N."* The contrapositive of this discovery, *"If for a given number P there is a number N such that P does not divide N^P-N, then P is a composite number,"* if true, would provide a useful test for primality. Fermat often left his discoveries unjustified, leaving the proof for others. This discovery was important enough to be given the title *Fermat's Little Theorem* to distinguish it from Fermat's Last Theorem.

The following two charts are the results of two spreadsheets: one that uses a few prime-divisors, and another that uses a few composite-divisors to illustrate

Fermat's Little Theorem: *"If P is a prime number and N any natural number then N^P-N is a multiple by P."*

QUOTIENTS when N^P-N is divided by P.

N/P	2	3	5	7	11	13
2	1	2	6	18	186	630
3	3	8	48	312	16104	122640
4	6	20	204	2340	381300	5162220
5	10	40	624	11160	4438920	93900240
6	15	70	1554	39990	32981550	1004668770
7	21	112	3360	117648	179756976	7453000800
8	28	168	6552	299592	780903144	42288908760

The prime-divisors 2, 3, 5, 7, 11, and 13 are used above. The absence of decimals indicates divisibility. This sheet reveals the quotient 40 when 5^3-5 =125-5=120 is divided by 3.

QUOTIENTS when N^P-N is by divided P.

N/P	2	4	6	8	9
2	1	3.5	10.33	31.75	56.667
3	3	19.5	121	819.75	2186.667
4	6	63	682	8191.5	29126.667
5	10	155	2603.33	48827.5	217013.33

The composite divisors 2, 4, 6, 8, and 9 are used above. This sheet reveals the quotient 31.75 when $2^8-2=256-2=254$ is divided by 8. In the case of The Little Theorem, Fermat had guessed correctly, but sometimes Fermat guessed incorrectly. He had a deep desire to find a formula that would produce prime numbers. Marin Mersenne (1588 – 1648), a friar also interested in mathematics, was collecting and recording mathematical discoveries sent to him by others. Mersenne thought that perhaps the formula 2^N-1 might produce prime numbers and communicated his idea to Fermat. Mersenne was incorrect, but Fermat thought that if N is a prime number, the formula would more likely produce prime numbers. The formula worked for the prime numbers 2, 3, 5, and 7, but failed for the prime number 11.

Mersenne is given credit for getting the search started and today prime numbers of the form 2^N-1 are called Mersenne Primes. Several are shown in the table below.

N	2^N-1	Prime Factor	Prime Factor
2	3		
3	7		
5	31		
7	127		
11	2047	23	89
13	8191		
17	131071		
19	524287		

Mersenne must have learned that some of his proposed numbers were not prime numbers, but he continued to be convinced that his formula would produce very large prime numbers. He asserted, without proof, that $2^{67}-1$ is a prime number.

In 1905, some 250 years after Mersenne, Frank Cole of Columbia University made a presentation at a math conference where, without saying a word, he wrote the powers of 2 (2, 4, 8, 16, etc.), all the way to 2^{67} on the left blackboard. He then subtracted the number 1 from 2^{67} and wrote the answer 147573952589676412927 on the same board.

On the right black board Cole wrote two numbers, 193707721 and 761838257287. He then proceeded to multiply them, arriving at 147573952589676412927, the same 21-digit number he had written on the left board. He then quietly replaced the chalk and returned to his seat. Mathematicians in the room suddenly realized that Cole had just demonstrated that $2^{67}-1$ is not a prime number. Mersenne had guessed wrong. Cole was given a standing ovation, a rare response at a convention of mathematicians.

The two factors, 193707721 and 761838257287 of the 21-digit number, are both prime numbers. In 1905, there were no computers to assist him, so I wonder how Cole arrived at these two prime factors?

As Fermat continued his search for a formula that would produce prime numbers, he became convinced that numbers of the form 2N2 +1 would do the ck. His formula is correct for the numbers 1, 2, 3, and 4. These four examples apparently convinced Fermat that for every number N, the formula would produce a prime number. Authors of the history of mathematics seem to agree that Fermat died without knowing he was mistaken. Perhaps Fermat was very mistaken, because mathematicians have yet to find any Fermat primes beyond $65537=2^24+1=2^{16}+1$.

Until recently, number theory had no practical use. As people began to transmit sensitive information over the internet, there was a need to keep the information secret and unreadable by all but the intended receiver. Because of Fermat's discoveries, large prime numbers were available to help fill that need.

When information is now transmitted electronically, a numerical key consisting of two very large prime numbers is used to encrypt the information. To read the information one must know the numerical key to decrypt it. The two prime numbers used in the key are so large that, for all practical purposes, they cannot be discovered, and are known only by the computer belonging to the intended receiver. In this way, large prime numbers provide internet security.

> *"One cannot escape the feeling that these mathematical formulas have an independent existence and an intelligence of their own, that they are wiser than we are, wiser ven than their discoverers."*
> —*Heinrich Hertz*

3.4 Euler's Proof of Fermat's Little Theorem

About the time of Fermat's death, Sir Isaac Newton (1642 – 1727) proved the Binomial Theorem, an algorithm which provided for the numbers in Pascal's triangle. These numbers give the coefficients when powers of sums and differences are expanded.

```
                    1
                 1     1
              1     2     1
           1     3     3     1
        1     4     6     4     1
     1     5    10    10     5     1
  1     6    15    20    15     6     1
1    7    21    35    35    21     7     1
```

I will illustrate by expanding the expressions $(X+1)^0$, $(X+1)^1$, $(X+1)^2$,

$(X+1)^3$, $(X+1)^4$, $(X+1)^5$, $(X+1)^6$, and $(X+1)^7$. By repeated multiplication we get the following results from algebra:

$(X+1)^0=1$ $(X+1)^1=1X+1$
$(X+1)^2=X^2+2X+1$
$(X+1)^3=X^3+3X^2+3X+1$
$(X+1)^4=X^4+4X^3+6X^2+4X+1$
$(X+1)^5=X^5+5X^4+10X^3+10X^2+5X+1$
$(X+1)^6=X^6+6X^5+15X^4+20X^3+15X^2+6X+1$
$(X+1)^7=X^7+7X^6+21X^5+35X^4+35X^3+21X^2+7X+1$

The formula for the coefficient of X^N in the expansion of $(X+1)^M$, where $N:::;M$ is M. For example the coefficient of X^3 in the ex (M-) pansion of $(X+1)^7$ equals 3 4 6 5 4 3 2 1 (3 2 1)(4 3 2 1) ^{65} 3s. Newton 3 2 1 discovered that when P is a prime number then the expansion of $(X+1)^P$ equals X^P+1+PK for some number K that depended only on the value of X. For example the expansion of $(X+1)^7=X^7+1+(7X^6+21X^5+35X^4+35X^3+21X^2+7X)$

So $(X+1)^7=X^7+1+7(X^6+3\ X^5+5\ X^4+5\ X^3+3\ X^2+X)$

In 1736 Leonhard Euler (1707 – 1783) used Newton's discovery to prove Fermat's Little Theorem: *"If P is a prime number then for every number N, N^P-N is a multiple of P."*

Proof by induction: Let P represent an arbitrary prime number and let S be the collection of all numbers N for which N^P-N is a multiple of P. Since $1^P-1=0$ it is a multiple of P and hence S contains 1. We now show that if S contains N, it will also contain N+1.

From S containing N we have $N^P-N=PQ$ for some number Q. From Newton's discovery we also have $(N+1)^P=N^P+1+PK$ for some number K. Subtracting N+1 from both sides of this equation gives us $(N+1)^P-(N+1)=(N^P+1+PK)-(N+1)=PK+N^P-N=PK+PQ$, a multiple of P. So S contains N+1. 25

In 1732 Euler discovered that 2 +1 is not a prime number because it equals $1+2^{32}=4294967297=641*6700417$. This was the first counter example to Fermat's formula $2+1$ for producing prime numbers.

Euler also added many more pairs of friendly numbers to the list of the only three known until his time.

Just as Euler found that Fermat once guessed wrong, future mathematicians found that Euler once guessed wrong. Fermat had shown that the equation $a^3+b^3=c^3$ had no solutions. Euler noted that the equation $a^3+b^3+c^3=d^3$ does, because $(3^3+4^3+5^3=6^3)$. Euler then claimed that equations such as, $a^4+b^4+c^4=d^4$, $a^5+b^5+c^5+d^5=e^5$, $a^6+b^6+c^6+d^6+e^6=f^6$, etc. would have no solutions. To generalize, Euler attempted to improve on Fermat's theorem by asserting that the number of variables needs to be at least one more than the powers to get even one solution.

In the twentieth century, mathematicians found that Euler's assertion was false. Below are two counter examples.

$95800^4+217519^4+414560^4=422481^4$
$27^5+84^5+110^5+133^5=144^5$.

We should judge Euler kindly, because computers were needed to find these examples. Moreover, Euler made many contributions to number theory and other areas of mathematics, such as infinite series, differential equations, and probability. The base of natural logarithms is denoted by the letter e in honor of Euler's many contributions to mathematics.

> *"I mean the word proof not in the sense of the lawyers, who set two half proofs equal to a whole one, but in the sense of a mathematician, where half proof = 0, and it is demanded for proof that every doubt becomes impossible."*
> —*Karl Friedrich Gauss*

3.5 Gauss and the Prime Number Theorem

Mathematicians who came after Fermat were very interested in prime numbers. Although they had no formula that would produce them all, other searches were created to provide insight into the nature of these important numbers. One of these searches was started by a woman, a rarity in mathematics before 1900. Sophie Germain (1776 – 1831) discovered another special collection of prime numbers that can be formulated. In the table below, notice how adding 1 to the double of some prime numbers is also a prime number. Today we call such numbers *Sophie Germain Primes*. For the prime number 2 we have 2*2+1=5, so 2 is a Germain prime. Likewise 2*3+1=7, and 2*5+1=11, and 2*11+1=23, and 2*23+1=47 are all prime numbers, so the prime numbers 2, 3, 5, 11, and 23 are Germain primes.

The prime numbers 7, 13, 17, 19, 31 and 37 are not Germain primes because 2*7+1=15, and 2*13+1=27, and 2*17+1=35, and 2*19+1=39, and 2*31+1=63, and 2*37+1=75 are all composite numbers.

	Prime	2P+1	Factor	Factor
G	*2*	*5*		
G	*3*	*7*		
G	*5*	*11*		
	7	*15*	*3*	*5*
G	*11*	*23*		
	13	*27*	*3*	
	17	*35*	*5*	*7*
	19	*39*	*3*	*13*
G	*23*	*47*		
G	*29*	*59*		
	31	*63*	*3*	*7*
	37	*75*	*3*	*5*
G	*41*	*83*		

These special prime numbers can be very large, as large as

92305*2^16998+1 which consists of 5,122 digits. Germain was very interested in Fermat's Last Theorem "*For every natural number N greater than 2, equations of the form $a^N+b^N=c^N$, have no solutions,*" and proved that the theorem is true when the power N is a Germain prime.

Carl Friedrich Gauss (1777 – 1855) added to our understanding of numbers and made many significant contributions to other areas of mathematics. When he made a discovery, he published it only after he had a proof and after he had developed the idea completely. One published result was the Fundamental Theorem of Algebra. It regards the number of solutions to polynomial equations that high school students are asked to solve.

Gauss also had a private diary, one in which he wrote some of his discoveries that he did not intend to share. Perhaps he was reluctant to make them public for fear that others would discover related theorems before he had time to fully develop the ideas. After his death, his diary was discovered and revealed that he had an interest in *triangular numbers*. Consider the following triangular shapes of dots:

```
  •          •          •          •
 • •        • •        • •        • •
           • • •      • • •      • • •
                     • • • •    • • • •
                                • • • • •
```

The quantity of these dots, 3, 6, 10, and 15 are called *triangular numbers*. When he was only ten years of age, Gauss discovered a formula that gives the sum of the first N numbers, beginning with 1 (i.e 1+2+3+4+...+N). His formula is (+1). This same formula gives the 2 triangular numbers. With N=100, the formula gives 5050 as a triangle number as well as the sum of the numbers from 1 to 100.

Gauss's diary reveals that in 1796, he discovered that *every number can be expressed as the sum of three triangular numbers*, not an easy statement to prove.

At the age of fourteen, Gauss obtain a math book that contained a table of logarithms. On one of those pages he wrote the German expression "Primzahlen unter a^a " with which math historians believe la Gauss anticipated the Prime Number Theorem.

Although no formula could be found to produce prime numbers, mathematicians are interested in how prime numbers are distributed among the collection of numbers. For example, given a number N, what is the proportion of prime numbers less than N? Another way to express this is to ask "If a number less number N is chosen randomly, what is the probability that the chosen number is a prime number?"

To provide some insight into the distribution of prime numbers among all the numbers, Gauss, like many other mathematicians, calculated the number of prime numbers less than a given number. For example, in Chapter 2 we saw that there are 25 prime numbers less than 100.

Mathematicians use the notation $\pi(N)$ to denote the number of prime numbers less than N. The table below shows the number and percent of prime numbers less than N for various values of N.

N	Pi(N)	% of Primes
1000	168	16.8
10,000	1,229	12.29
100,000	9,592	9.592
1,000,000	78,498	7.8498
10,000,000	664,579	6.6458
100,000,000	5,761,455	5.7615

Mathematicians eventually discovered that Ln( ) is a formula that approximates the values of $\pi(N)$, a discovery known as the Prime Number Theorem. More recently, they improved the formula to ___ -_____, where Ln(x) denotes logarithms base e. See the table below:

[Ln( )-1)

N	N/Ln(N)	N/(Ln(N)-1)	Pi(N)
1000	144	169	168
10,000	1,085	1,217	1,229
100,000	8,685	9,512	9,592
1,000,000	72,382	78,030	78,498
10,000,000	620,420	661,458	664,579
100,000,000	5,428,681	5,740,303	5,761,455

The story of prime numbers is not finished. In 1859, Bernhard Riemann proposed a conjecture that contains implications regarding the distribution of prime numbers. His conjecture, known as the **Riemann Hypothesis**, is today the most important unsolved problem in mathematics. The conjecture is difficult to state, and beyond the scope of this book. It is also beyond the comprehension of this author.

In the next chapter I turn my attention to a math problem that I do understand. Perhaps I am the first person to bring the problem to the attention of mathematicians. You will learn why I challenge them to solve the problem.

> "The formulation of the problem is often more essential than its solution...."
> — **Albert Einstein**

Chapter Four
The Holy Grail of Mathematics

4.1 Description of a Pythagorean Box

The Holy Grail of mathematics is a Pythagorean Box, a rectangular box where the length of each edge and each diagonal on the faces and inside the box are natural numbers.

I cannot recall where I got the idea of this special box. A rectangular box consists of six rectangular faces with opposite faces congruent. Each face has two congruent diagonals. A rectangular box also has four congruent diagonals inside, running from a corner of a face to the opposite corner of the opposite face. Each diagonal is the hypotenuse of a right triangle.

For reference and description, I use upper case letters A, B, C, D, E, F, G, and H to label the eight vertices of the box. I use the seven lower case letters t, u, v, w, x, y, and z to denote the length of the edges and diagonals. (See figures on next page.)

Angles BAD, CBF, and GHD are right angles, so the sides t, u, and w, the sides u, v, and x, and the sides t, v, and y satisfy the Pythagorean equations $t^2+u^2=w^2$, $u^2+v^2=x^2$, and $t^2+v^2=y^2$.

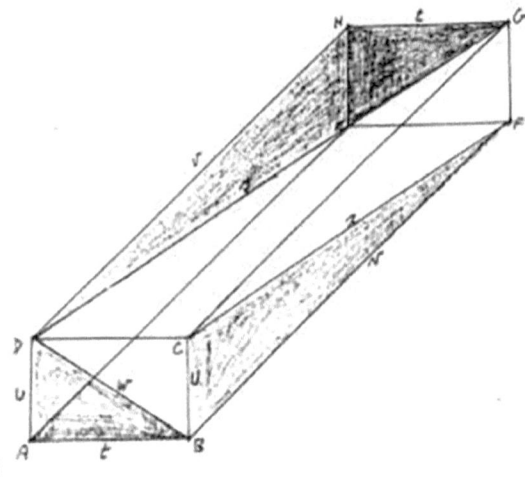

Figure 1

The rectangular sides HGFE and EFBA are mutually perpendicular, so HEB is a right triangle, and hence the sides u, y, and z satisfy the Pythagorean equation $u^2+y^2=z^2$.

Likewise the rectangular sides BADC and BCGF are mutually perpendicular, so DCF is a right triangle and hence the sides t, x, and z satisfy the Pythagorean equation $t^2+x^2=z^2$.

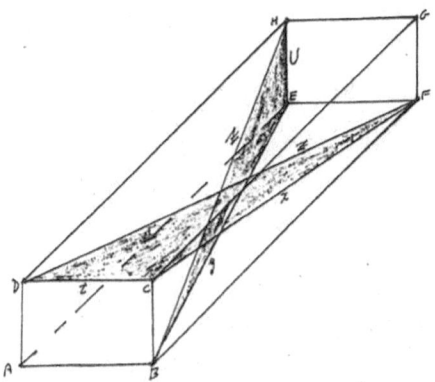

Figure 2

The rectangular sides ABCD and ABFE are mutually perpendicular, so DBF is a right angle and hence the sides w, v, and z satisfy the Pythagorean equation $w^2+v^2=z^2$.

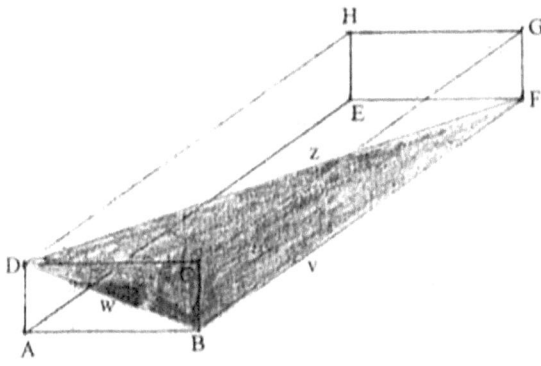

Figure 3

The six Pythagorean triples yield **six** equations with seven variables.

$$t^2+u^2=w^2 \qquad t^2+v^2=y^2 \qquad u^2+y^2=z^2$$
$$w^2+v^2=z^2 \qquad t^2+x^2=z^2 \qquad u^2+v^2=x^2$$

From $u^2+t^2=w^2$ we have $u^2=w^2-t^2$ and from $w^2+v^2=z^2$ we have $v^2=z^2-w^2$, so $u^2+v^2=(w^2-t^2)+(z^2-w^2)=z^2-t^2$. Then from $t^2+x^2=z^2$, we have $z^2-t^2=x^2$.

Thus the equation $u^2+v^2=x^2$ follows from the other five and the system can be reduced to the **five** equations:

$$t^2+u^2=w^2 \quad t^2+v^2=y^2 \quad w^2+v^2=z^2 \quad t^2+x^2=z^2 \quad u^2+y^2=z^2$$

From $t^2+u^2=w^2$ we have $u^2=w^2-t^2$ and $y^2=t^2-v^2$ so $u^2+y^2=(w^2-t^2)+(t^2+v^2)$ which is w^2+v^2 which equals z^2.

Thus the equation $w^2+v^2=z^2$ follows from the other four and the system can be reduced to the following **four** equations:

$$t^2+u^2=w^2 \qquad t^2+v^2=y^2 \qquad t^2+x^2=z^2 \qquad u^2+y^2=z^2$$

To find the Holy Grail of Mathematics is to find seven natural numbers, t, u, v, w, x, y, and z that simultaneously satisfy these four equations. The numbers come in threes, which are called Pythagorean triples. I introduced these numbers In Chapter 2 because Fermat used their properties in one of his proofs.

The notation A-B-C identifies a Pythagorean triple. An unlimited number of triples can be found by substituting two numbers X and Y, with X<Y, into the formulas $A=Y^2-X^2$, $B=2XY$, and $C=\sqrt{Y2 + X2}$.

> "The real danger is not that computers will think like men, but that men will begin to think like computers."
> —Sydney J. Harris

4.2 Searching for the Holy Grail of Mathematics

To search for solutions to the four equations, I created a spreadsheet that could test three groups of Pythagorean triples.

t	u	T	U	W
3	4	105	140	175
5	12	105	252	273
t	x	T	X	Z
7	24	105	360	375
		U	Y	X
		140	273	306,80

The formulas in this spreadsheet used $T = t_1 \ast t_2 \ast t_3 = 3 \ast 5 \ast 7 = 105$ and $U = u \ast t_2 \ast t_3 = 4 \ast 5 \ast 7 = 140$ in the third column.

It used $V = v*t_1*t_3 = 12*3*7 = 252$ and $X = x*t_1*t_2 = 24*3*5 = 360$ in the fourth column.

In the fifth column I used the formulas

$$W = \sqrt{T2 + U2} \qquad Y = \sqrt{T2 + v2}$$

$$Z = \sqrt{T2 + X2} \qquad X = \sqrt{U2 + v2}$$

Valid dimensions of a Pythagorean Box will occur when the two X's have the same values; therefore, the trial above failed. Four more trials are shown below. Each trial failed to produce a Pythagorean Box.

t	u	T	U	W		t	u	T	U	W
5	12	315	756	819		7	24	693	2376	2475
t	v	T	V	Y		t	v	T	V	Y
7	24	315	1080	1125		9	40	693	3080	3157
t	x	T	X	Z		t	x	T	X	Z
9	40	315	1400	1435		11	60	693	3780	3843
		U	Y	X				U	Y	X
		756	1125	1355.42				2376	3157	3951.21

t	u	T	U	W		t	u	T	U	W
3	4	189	252	315		5	12	495	1188	1287
t	v	T	V	Y		t	v	T	V	Y
7	24	189	648	675		9	40	495	2200	2255
t	x	T	X	Z		t	x	T	X	Z
9	40	189	840	861		11	60	495	2700	2745
		U	Y	X				U	Y	X
		252	675	720.51				1188	2255	2548.80

I used this spreadsheet process with many different triples and each failed to produce a Pythagorean Box. One could automate the spreadsheet process with a computer program to search for the dimensions of a Pythagorean Box, but I suspect that a Pythagorean Box does not exist, so I present the following as McCabe's Conjecture: *"The Holy Grail of Mathematics will never be found."* (not even by Harrison Ford).

> *"It would be very discouraging if somewhere down the line you could ask a computer if the Riemann Hypothesis is correct and it said, 'Yes, it is true, but you won't be able to understand the proof.'"*
> —Ronald Graham

CHAPTER FIVE

The Unknown and the Unknowable

5.1 Hilbert's Program

How many ways can a family have four children? We can arrive at the answer by listing each possibility. If we let B represent a boy and let G represent a girl, then the list without regard to the order of their birth is: BBBB, BBBG, BBGG, BGGG, and GGGG. So the answer is five. Each child in a family with four children will have three siblings. These are mathematical facts, verifiable each day by each child as he or she counts her brothers and sisters. But the counts four, five, and three symbolized by 4, 5, and 3 respectively are, by themselves, devoid of a single context. Mathematicians say that 4, 5, and 3 are counting numbers and need to ask, "What is a counting number?" Asking this question places them in the same situation faced by Euclid when he asked the questions "What is a point? What is a line?" Euclid was cautious and wise enough not to define a point and a line. Rather, he focused on the required properties that his perceived points and lines seemed to have.

One of Euclid's perceptions was the following: "*Given a line and a point not on the line, there is one and only one line through the point that is parallel to the given line.*" A statement equivalent to this one became

Euclid's famous Fifth Postulate. Why do we now call it a postulate rather than an axiom?

An axiom is supposed to be self-evident, while a postulate is a statement whose truth is simply accepted without question. It turns out that Euclid's Fifth was not so self-evident. Mathematicians accepted Euclid's first four axioms without question and later, as mathematicians attempted to prove the Fifth Axiom using logic and the first four, they made surprising discoveries.

In the early 1800s, mathematicians were able to prove that there are three geometries, each satisfying the first four axioms of Euclid, but each with a different answer to the question *"Given a line and a point P not on the line, how many lines containing P are parallel to the given line?"* Euclid had asserted that *"there is one and only one line through the point that is also parallel to the given line."* Two mathematicians, Janos Bolyai (1802 – 1860) and Nikolai Lobachevsky (1792 – 1856), independently discovered a geometry that satisfied the first four axioms, but where *"there are an infinity of lines through the point that are parallel to the given line."* This non-Euclidean geometry is known as hyperbolic geometry.

In 1854 Bernhard Riemann discovered elliptical geometry, where *"there are no lines through the point that are parallel to the given line."* These other geometries were shown to be just as consistent as the one perceived by Euclid. Although we seem to live in a Euclidean world, perhaps the universe is non-Euclidean.

This surprising result in geometry caused uncertainties regarding arithmetic. What is arithmetic? Can we find axioms that reduce arithmetic to symbols where truth is not the result of experience and intuition, but rather the result of formal logic applied to the properties of the symbols?

In the late seventeenth century, two mathematicians provided the required axioms. Giuseppe Peano (1858 – 1932) made slight improvements to axioms proposed by Richard Dedekind (1831 – 1916). The axioms are based on the properties of the numbers we use for counting, and reflect the notion of equality and the operation we know as adding. See **Appendix G** for a discussion of **Dedekind – Peano Axiomatic Arithmetic.**

Peano and other mathematicians used the axioms to develop a theory that was intended to accurately reflect the arithmetic we use daily. A proof of consistency was provided for the theory, and then mathematicians began to raise important questions regarding this axiomatic theory. *"Do the axioms capture all that is true in the arithmetic we had in mind when the axioms were proposed? If not, what axioms shall be added to capture all that is true in arithmetic?"*

Related to these questions, David Hilbert (1862 – 1943), who had already proposed a stronger set of postulates for the geometry of Euclid, challenged his fellow mathematicians to create axiomatic systems that would eliminate theoretical uncertainties from all of mathematics. His challenge was delivered on August 8, 1900 at the International Congress of Mathematicians, held at the Sorbonne in Paris.

In his speech, Hilbert identified ten important mathematics problems, and in a later paper he identified another thirteen. He challenged mathematicians to solve these problems over the next few decades. Two of these problems, Goldbach's Conjecture and the Twin Prime Conjecture, can be understood by almost anyone, and each will be discussed further on. Hilbert identified the need for a proof of consistency for any proposed set of axioms of arithmetic. It is likely that Peano attended the speech and was pleased to learn that his axioms would most likely contribute to what was to become known as Hilbert's Program.

Hilbert told his audience that he believed that every mathematical problem should have a solution--or at least a proof than no solution existed. He sought a theory of arithmetic where every true statement could be proved. Further on we will learn that Hilbert was much too optimistic regarding the power of a formal axiomatic theory of arithmetic.

> *"Proof is the idol before whom the pure mathematician tortures himself."*
> —*Sir Arthur Eddington*

5.2 Goldbach's Conjectures

A conjecture in arithmetic is a statement about a collection of numbers that appears to be true, yet remains unproven. A conjecture is a guess that can be refuted with one counterexample. There are many conjectures regarding arithmetic. The statement that there are an infinite number of twin primes is a conjecture. Fermat's Last Theorem was a conjecture until Andrew Wiles discovered his proof.

Christian Goldbach (1690 - 1764) was a German mathematician born in Konigsberg, a part of Prussia. Other famous mathematicians living in his time included Nicholas Bernoulli (1687 – 1726), Gottfried Leibniz (1646 – 1716), Sir Isaac Newton (1642 – 1727), and Leonhard Euler (1707 – 1783). Goldbach often corresponded with Euler regarding his mathematical research.

In 1742, while working at the Russian Ministry of Foreign Affairs in St. Petersburg, Russia, Goldbach discovered several theorems regarding sums of prime numbers. In a letter to Euler, Goldbach stated his now famous conjecture: *"Every even number greater than 4 can be expressed as the sum of two primes."*

To explore Goldbach's conjecture, I wrote a computer program that used my file of prime numbers to search for pairs of prime numbers that would sum to a given even number. For every even number between 4 and 209,458, the program found two prime numbers that summed to the number. The program was limited because 104,729 is the largest prime number in the file.

I had written an earlier version of the program that found several pairs of prime numbers that summed to a given even number. For example, 100 is the sum of 3 and 97, the sum of 11 and 89, the sum of 17 and 83, the sum of 29 and 71, the sum of 41 and 59, as well as the sum of 47 and 53. My current program finds the two primes with the smallest difference which sum to a given even number (100=47+53).

I modified my program to explore even numbers that can be expressed as the difference of two prime numbers. The evidence I collected suggested the following, "*If an even number E is expressible as the sum of two prime numbers, then E can be expressed as the difference of two prime numbers.*" My proof of this theorem first requires the proof of **Theorem F**: "*For any odd number O, there is an even number E such that O+E is a prime number.*"

Proof of **Theorem F**: For a given odd number O and every number J, O+2J is an odd number. Because there is no largest prime number, let Q represent the next prime after O. The prime number Q is odd and is therefore equal to O+2J for some number J. The even number 2J is the required even number.

Proof of the theorem "*If an even number E is expressible as the sum of two prime numbers, then E can be expressed as the difference of two prime numbers.*" Let $E=P_1+P_2$ where $P_1 < P_2$, then $E-P_2$ is an odd number.

Let J be a number and let S be the collection of all numbers of the form $E-P_2+2J$. The collection S contains all <u>odd</u> numbers larger than $E-P_2$, thus all <u>prime</u> numbers larger than $E-P_2$.

Let K be a number and let T be the collection of all numbers of the form P_1+2K. The collection T contains all odd numbers larger than P_1, thus all prime numbers larger than P_1. Notice that P_1+E is an element of T.

The collection T is a subset of the collection S. From **Theorem F** we can choose an even number E_1 so that both $P_3=E-P_2+E_1$ and $P_4=P_1+E+E_1$ are prime numbers. Then $P_4-P_3=(P_1+E+E_1)-(E-P_2+E_1)$ or $P_4-P_3=P_1+P_2+E-E+E_1-E_1$. So $P_4-P_3=P_1+P_2=E$.

Is Goldbach's conjecture true? On one side of the question, mathematicians have used very powerful computers to search for a counter-example, i.e. an even number that cannot be expressed as a sum of two prime numbers. To date no counterexample has been found. On the other side of the question, they have attempted unsuccessfully to discover a proof of Goldbach's Conjecture. In 1931, the situation became more muddled.

At the age of twenty-five, mathematician Kurt Godel (1906 – 1978) discovered that the axiomatic arithmetic of Peano and Dedekind was not sufficient to prove all true arithmetic statements. He then went on to prove a more startling theorem. Godel showed that adding more axioms to the nine that Peano and Dedekind proposed would still leave some statements in an undecidable state, perhaps true, perhaps false.

Godel's discovery occurred ten years before Hilbert's death. It is called the **Incompleteness Theorem** and reveals that no finite axiomatic system can capture all that is true in arithmetic. When a theory is found to be incomplete, adding an axiom can possibly complete the theory. But adding an axiom to arithmetic is fraught with the danger of causing the axiom-appended arithmetic to become inconsistent. Consistency is an absolute requirement for any mathematical theory, for without it the theory would collapse like a house of cards.

Godel was able to prove that no matter what statement you add, self-evident or not, undecidable arithmetic statements will remain. Contrary to Hilbert's desire and belief, arithmetic will forever remain incomplete. In view of Godel's Incompleteness Theorem, the question regarding the truth of Goldbach's Conjecture might be forever undecidable. Perhaps it is true, but will forever be without a proof.

This Incompleteness Theorem could possibly discourage some mathematicians from attempting to discover proofs in arithmetic. But Andrew Wiles was not discouraged and persevered for eight years to achieve his proof of Fermat's Last Theorem, a case where passion for truth overcomes all obstacles.

Godel was born a German, but was raised in Austria in the time that World War I began and ended, a time when Hitler came to power in Nazi Germany. In the mid and late 1930s, Godel made several visits to the US. He attended math conferences, met his future friend Albert

Einstein, and gave a series of lectures at the Institute for Advanced Studies in Princeton, New Jersey.

Godel returned to Austria where, because of his friendships with his Jewish colleagues, he lost his university position. In 1939, World War II was underway and the German army found him fit for conscription. So like many disaffected Europeans, Godel fled his homeland. With his wife Adele, he traveled eastward through Siberia to the Pacific and sailed to the US from Japan.

In America, Godel landed a position at the Institute of Advanced Studies in New Jersey, where he spent the remainder of his life discussing mathematics and physics with his friend Albert Einstein.

As early as 1936, Godel showed signs of mental illness. He became afflicted with paranoia and developed a deep fear of being poisoned. Eventually Godel's fear of being poisoned led to his dependence on his wife to prepare his food. He would eat only what Adele had prepared. In 1977, Adele was hospitalized and Godel refused to eat. He too was eventually hospitalized, and died weighing only 65 pounds, a sad ending for an eccentric mathematical genius.

Further on we meet another mathematical genius who, although eccentric, found joy from life and brought enjoyment to many other mathematicians.

> *"The sciences, even the best — mathematics and astronomy — are like sportsmen, who seize whatever prey offers, even without being able to make any use of it."*
> *—Ralph Waldo Emerson*

5.3 Gaping at Gaps

To understand how the prime numbers are distributed among all the counting numbers, mathematicians have studied the size of the gaps between prime numbers. By the size of a gap we mean the number of consecutive composite numbers between two prime numbers. For example, between the prime numbers 89 and 97 are the seven consecutive composite numbers 90, 91, 92, 93, 94, 95, 96, so 7 is the gap size between the prime number 89 and the next prime number 97.

Accessing my file of 10,000 prime numbers, I wrote a computer program to study the largest gap size of the first 10, 100, 200, 500, 1000, 2000, 5000, and 10000 prime numbers. The results are shown below.

The 1st N prime numbers.	The largest gap size.
100	13
200	21
500	33
1000	33
2000	43
5000	71
10000	71

In the first 10000 prime numbers, only one pair of prime numbers, the 3387th prime number 31397 and the 3388th prime number 31469, had a gap size of 71.

Accessing my file of 10000 prime numbers, I wrote a computer program to count the quantity of each gap size 1 to 75. The results of my program are shown below.

GAP SIZE	COUNT	GAP SIZE	COUNT
1	1271	39	28
3	1263	41	20
5	2012	43	5
7	801	45	6
9	953	47	3
11	1008	49	5
13	512	51	8
15	353	53	5
17	537	55	1
19	249	57	4
21	235	59	2
23	222	61	1
25	91	63	1
27	102	65	0
29	154	67	0
31	35	69	0
33	36	71	1
35	55	73	0
37	20	75	0

You must wonder why there are no even gap sizes. Consider the situation where we have four consecutive numbers following a prime number P. Since P is odd it has the representation 2J-1, so the next five numbers have the representations 2J, 2J+1, 2J+2, 2J+3, 2J+4. But this last number, 2J+4 cannot be a prime number because it is a multiple of 2. For a proof in general we notice that the N consecutive numbers following an odd number 2J-1 can be represented by 2J, 2J+1, 2J+2, ..., 2J+(N-1). If N is an even number, then N-1 is an odd number, so the next number 2J+N is even and not a prime number. So N must always be an odd number.

It so happens that gap sizes can be arbitrarily large. Let me show you why. Consider the following sequence of five numbers 6!+2, 6!+3, 6!+4, 6!+5, 6!+6, where 6!=1*2*3*4*5*6. Then these five numbers are multiples of 2, 3, 4, 5, and 6 respectively. These five consecutive numbers 722, 724, 725, 726, 727 are all between the prime numbers 719 and 727.

In general the N consecutive composite numbers $(N+1)!+2, (N+1)!+3, (N+1)!+4, (N+1)!+5, \ldots, (N+1)!+(N+1)$ are all between two prime numbers.

An important question for mathematicians is *"Is there a gap size with an unbounded count?"* Asked in another manner the question becomes *"Is there a gap size that is repeated infinitely?"* When the gap size is 1 such as for the prime pairs 3 and 5, 5 and 7, as well as 11 and 13, the pair is called a twin prime. We next consider the infinitude of these pairs.

> *"I'll tell you once, and I'll tell you again.*
> *There's always a prime between n and 2n."*
> —*Poem by Paul Erdos*

5.4 The Twin-Prime Conjecture

Early mathematicians surmised that the number of twin primes is unlimited, and so we have the twin prime conjecture: *"The collection of pairs of prime numbers with exactly one composite number between them is infinite."*

My computer program identified 1271 twins among the first 10000 prime numbers. Below is a list of 42 twin primes.

3	5	197	199	641	643
5	7	227	229	659	661
11	13	239	241	809	811
17	19	269	271	821	823
29	31	281	283	827	829

41	43	311	313	857	859
59	61	347	349	881	883
71	73	419	421	1019	1021
101	103	431	433	031	1033
107	109	461	463	1049	1051
137	139	521	523	1061	1063
149	151	569	571	1091	1093
179	181	599	601	1151	1153
191	193	617	619	1229	1231

It seems that few properties have been discovered about twin primes. I will prove a simple one. *"If P and Q are numbers that differ by two, then one plus their product is a square number."*

Proof: Given Q–P=2, let Q=P+2, then substituting P+2 for Q in the expression 1+PQ results in the expression 1+P(P+2). With algebra we have $1+P(P+2)=1+P^2+2P=P^2+2P+1=(P+1)^2$.

The above theorem leads to a corollary: *"If P and P+2 are a pair of twin primes then 1 plus their product is a square number."*

Here is another theorem regarding twin primes: *"The smallest prime number of a twin prime pair is of the form 6Q-1 for some quotient Q."*

Proof: To begin note that dividing any number by 6 results in one of only six remainders, namely 0, 1, 2, 3, 4, or 5. If the number being divided by 6 is odd, then this list of remainders is reduced to 1, 3, or 5.

Dividing the smallest prime number P of a twin prime pair by 6 cannot leave a remainder of 1, because if it did, P would be of the form 6J+1 and the larger prime of the pair, P+2 would equal (6J+1)+2=6J+3, a multiple of 3, contrary to fact that P+2 is a prime number.

Likewise, dividing the smallest prime number P of a twin prime pair by 6 cannot leave a remainder of 3, because if it did, P would be of the form 6J+3, a multiple of 3 and thus not a prime number. Therefore P must be of the form 6J+5, where 6J+5 equals 6J+(6-1)=6(J+1)-1=6Q-1.

The above logic leads to the conclusion that twin primes are always of the form 6Q-1 and 6Q+1. We cannot conclude that numbers of the form 6Q-1 are prime numbers. The composite number 35, which equals 6*6-1 provides a counter example. Nor can we conclude that when 6Q-1 is a prime number, the next odd number is necessarily a prime number. Here the numbers 23 and 25 provide a counter example (23=6*4-1 while 23+2=25.)

In 1845, French mathematician Joseph Bertrand (1822–1900) conjectured, *"For every number N there is at least one prime number between N and 2N."* In 1850, the Russian mathematician Pafnuty Chebyshev (1821–1894) proved Bertrand's conjecture. Then, at the age of 19, the Hungarian mathematician Paul Erdos (1913-1996) provided a much simpler proof of Bertrand's conjecture.

Erdos' simpler proof is typical of mathematical progress where a young mathematician improves or enhances an earlier mathematician's work. His proof and further discoveries led to the recognition by mathematicians everywhere that Erdos (pronounced *air-dish*) was a mathematical genius. He is, by far, the most interesting mathematician I have ever learned about.

Imagine that you are a research mathematician at some university, the phone rings, and Erdos explains he is at the bus station and requests that you give him a ride to your home because he wants to stay as your guest for a few days. You are familiar with this man and what he has to offer, so you quickly agree.

On the way to your home he talks math, primarily about your research area. For several days you provide Erdos with room and board, and in return he makes suggestions that enable you both to discover a proof of a theorem. You are grateful for his help and you drive Erdos back to the bus station from which he is off to visit some other mathematician. During the next month you write and submit a mathematical paper to a professional journal, under both Erdos' name and your name. The paper is accepted and soon published in the journal. This scenario happened again and again, both here in the US and in several other countries. Consistent with this unusual practice, Erdos had a saying, *"Another roof, another proof."*

Since his early days in Hungary, Erdos had offers from several universities, but he never accepted a permanent position at any of them. He never owned a car or a home. He never had a romantic relationship and was celibate his whole life.

Erdos traveled with a small suitcase and his math notebooks. His suitcase contained a couple changes of clothes that were often washed by his hosts. Ronald Graham, a special friend and fellow mathematician, helped Erdos with his taxes and banking needs.

Erdos had a great sense of humor and was a showman of sorts. He was extraordinarily generous with the small amount of money he did earn. He collected stipends from talks he gave, and he earned prize money for problems he solved. One year Erdos won the Wolf Prize of $50,000 and eventually gave much of it away to charity.

During much of his life, Erdos was free to travel throughout the world where he attended math conferences, gave lectures at universities, and visited his many friends who were also research mathematicians. After earning his PhD in 1934, he left Hungary for a post-graduate position at Manchester in England. He was there until 1938 when he left for a fellowship position at the Institute for Advanced Studies in Princeton, NJ. A year or so later he attempted to join his friends at Los Alamos who were working on the Manhattan Project to produce the first atomic bomb. He was refused a position.

In 1943 Erdos accepted a part-time position at Purdue University. In 1948 he returned to his home in Hungary but left hurriedly in 1949 because of Stalin's plan to close the borders. During the three years, 1949 to 1952, he traveled between England and the US several times. In 1952, Erdos landed a position at Notre Dame in Indiana, a university that gave him some freedom to interrupt his teaching to visit with mathematicians around the US.

In 1954, Erdos was invited to a math conference in Amsterdam, but the US would not issue him a re-entry permit. This refusal was due in part because he was from a communist country, and they feared he might return there. He left for Amsterdam without the permit and spent the next eight years traveling throughout Europe, including a three-month position at Hebrew University in Israel. After Stalin died, Erdos made several visits to Hungary where his mother, Anna, still resided.

In 1959, the US allowed Erdos to attend a math conference in Denver, provided he would leave the country as soon as the conference was over. In 1963, after more than a hundred mathematicians petitioned the US State Department, Erdos was allowed to return. In 1976 he made a visit to the Institute for Advanced Studies where he met both Kurt Godel and Albert Einstein. It was a time when Godel was having a crisis of confidence, and like Einstein, Erdos tried to provide Godel with encouragement.

Erdos had math friends everywhere, including 485 with whom he wrote at least one published paper. He wrote or co-authored more than 1400 academic papers. Erdos was the epitome of one with a passion for numbers.

I felt the need to share this delightful human being with my readers. I learned about him while reading Paul Hoffman's *The Man Who Loved Only Numbers*. I must now get back to his theorem "*For every number N there is at least one prime number between N and 2N.*"

It occurred to me that perhaps somewhere between every number N and its double there is a twin prime, and so I wrote a computer program to investigate this possibility. My program found at least one pair of twins between N and 2N for every number N from 3 to 104500. I now feel safe in proposing an alternative Twin-Prime Conjecture: "*For every number N>3, there is at least one pair of twin primes between N and 2N.*" Now if only Erdos was here to help me prove the conjecture.

For my next discussion, I need to restate **Theorem F**: "*For any odd number O, there is an even number E such that O+E is a prime number.*"

To attack the Twin-Prime Conjecture, suppose there is a largest pair of prime numbers P and Q=P+2. For the supposed largest prime number P, let S_p represent the set of all numbers J such that P+2J is a prime number. **Theorem F** assures us that S_p is not empty, in fact we know that the set S_p is an infinite set. Likewise for the prime number Q (the twin of P) let S_Q represent the set of all numbers K such that Q+2K is a prime number. Again **Theorem F** assures us that S_Q is not empty.

If there is a number L contained in both sets S_P and S_Q, then both P+2L and Q+2L are prime numbers with a difference (Q+2L)-(P+2L)=Q-P=2. This would contradict our choice of the largest pair of twin primes. But that **If** at the beginning of the previous sentence is a **big If** indeed, for if we could somehow prove the existence of L, we would have an indirect proof of the Twin-Prime Conjecture.

I include this reasoning to show that there are different approaches one might take to discover a proof of the elusive proposition "*There are an infinite quantity of pairs of prime numbers that differ by 2.*"

In ending this story about numbers and proofs, I share reflections of three mathematicians. David Hilbert once remarked, "*If I were to awaken after having slept for a thousand years, my first question would be: Has the Riemann hypothesis been proven?*" Regarding problems that are easily stated but difficult to solve, Erdos is quoted as saying, "*A problem worthy of attack will prove its worth by fighting back.*" Ronald Graham, his close friend, has written, "*The trouble with integers is that we have examined only the small ones .... Our brains have evolved to get us out of the rain, find where the berries are, and keep us from getting killed. Our brains did not evolve to help us grasp large numbers or to look at things in a hundred thousand dimensions.*"

Appendix A

The numbers in the first column are divided by the numbers in the first row to produce the corresponding quotients and remainders.

	5		6		7	
	Quotient	Remainder	Quotient	Remainder	Quotient	Remainder
15	3	0	2	3	2	1
16	3	1	2	4	2	2
17	3	2	2	5	2	3
18	3	3	3	0	2	4
19	3	4	3	1	2	5
20	4	0	3	2	2	6
21	4	1	3	3	3	0
22	4	2	3	4	3	1
23	4	3	3	5	3	2
24	4	4	4	0	3	3
25	5	0	4	1	3	4

	5		6		7	
	Quotient	Remainder	Quotient	Remainder	Quotient	Remainder
15	=INT($A3/B$1)	=B$1*($A3/B$1-B3)	=INT($A3/E$1)	=E$1*($A3/E$1-E3)	=INT($A3/H$1)	=H$1*($A3/H$1-H3)
=A3+1	=INT($A4/B$1)	=B$1*($A4/B$1-B4)	=INT($A4/E$1)	=E$1*($A4/E$1-E4)	=INT($A4/H$1)	=H$1*($A4/H$1-H4)
=A4+1	=INT($A5/B$1)	=B$1*($A5/B$1-B5)	=INT($A5/E$1)	=E$1*($A5/E$1-E5)	=INT($A5/H$1)	=H$1*($A5/H$1-H5)
=A5+1	=INT($A6/B$1)	=B$1*($A6/B$1-B6)	=INT($A6/E$1)	=E$1*($A6/E$1-E6)	=INT($A6/H$1)	=H$1*($A6/H$1-H6)
=A6+1	=INT($A7/B$1)	=B$1*($A7/B$1-B7)	=INT($A7/E$1)	=E$1*($A7/E$1-E7)	=INT($A7/H$1)	=H$1*($A7/H$1-H7)
=A7+1	=INT($A8/B$1)	=B$1*($A8/B$1-B8)	=INT($A8/E$1)	=E$1*($A8/E$1-E8)	=INT($A8/H$1)	=H$1*($A8/H$1-H8)
=A8+1	=INT($A9/B$1)	=B$1*($A9/B$1-B9)	=INT($A9/E$1)	=E$1*($A9/E$1-E9)	=INT($A9/H$1)	=H$1*($A9/H$1-H9)

Appendix B

The spreadsheet calculates the individual digits of powers of 3 as well as the sums of these digits.

P	3^P	The digits of 3^P						Sum of the digits
1	3	3					=	3
2	9	9					=	9
3	27	2	7				=	9
4	81	8	1				=	9
5	243	2	4	3			=	9
6	729	7	2	9			=	18
7	2187	2	1	8	7		=	18
8	6561	6	5	6	1		=	18
9	19683	1	9	6	8	3	=	27
10	59049	5	9	0	4	9	=	27
11	177147	1	7	7	1	4	7	=	27
12	531441	5	3	1	4	4	1	=	18

P	3^P	The digits of 3^P				Sums
1	3	3			=	3
=A3+1	=3^A4	9			=	=SUM(C4:E4)
=A4+1	=3^A5	=INT(B5/10)	=B5-10*C5		=	=SUM(C5:E5)
=A5+1	=3^A6	=INT(B6/10)	=B6-10*C6		=	=SUM(C6:E6)
=A6+1	=3^A7	=INT(B7/10^2)	=INT(B7/10)-10*C7	=INT(B7)-10*INT(B7/10)	=	=SUM(C7:E7)
=A7+1	=3^A8	=INT(B8/100)	=INT(B8/10)-10*C8	=INT(B8)-10*INT(B8/10)	=	=SUM(C8:E8)

Appendix C

Adam's Algorithm

56 E = D*Q, D is largest odd divisor of E. L=(D-1)/2. S is the start of a consecutive sum. Q is the largest power of 2 that divides E. When Q>L start with Q-L, otherwise start with L-Q+1.

Q=Powers of 2	1	2	*3*	4	5	6	7	8
	2	4	8	16	32	64	128	256
D	28	14	*7*	3.5	1.75	0.88	0.44	0.22
L	14	6.5	1.25	0.375	-0.06	-0.28	-0.39	-0.445
Q-L	5	-2.5	*5*	14.75	31.63	64.06	128.3	256.4
L-Q+1	13	3.5	-4	-13.75	-30.63	-63.06	-127.3	-255.4
S	6	5	7	8	9	10	11	12
Sum	5	11	18	26	35	45	**56**	68

D		=ROUND($A1/B3,2)	=ROUND($A1/C3,2)		=ROUND($A1/D3,2)		=ROUND($A1/E3,2)	
L	=(B4-1)/2	=(C4-1)/2	=(D4-1)/2	=(E4-1)/2	=(F4-1)/2	=(G4-1)/2	=(H4-1)/2
Q-L	=D3-D5	=C3-C5	=D3-D5	=E3-E5	=F3-F5	=G3-G5	=H3-H5
L-Q+1	=B5-B3+1	=C5-C3+1	=D5-D3+1	=E5-E3+1	=F5-F3+1	=G5-G3+1	=H5-H3+1
S	5	=B8+1	=C8+1	=D8+1	=E8+1	=F8+1	=G8+1
Sum	=B8	=B9+C8	=C9+D8	=D9+E8	=E9+F8	=F9+G8	=G9+H8

Appendix D

Mutually Friendly Numbers

For the first sheet, the number 1184, in the top right corner is divided by the numbers 2, 4, 8, 16, 17, 18, 19, 20, 21 and 32, with the quotients shown in the second row. The 0's and 1's in the third row are the consequence of a logical IF statement [=IF(B2=INT(B2),1,0)] and serves to eliminate the decimal quotients in the second row. The numbers in the fourth row are the sum of the first three numbers in columns one through seven. The number 1210, in the bottom right corner is the sum of the numbers (1+594+300+156+90+69) in the fourth row.

	2	4	8	16	17	18	19	20	21	32	**_1184_**
	592	296	148	74	69.7	65.8	62.3	59.2	56	37	
	1	1	1	1	0	0	0	0	0	1	
1	594	300	156	90	0	0	0	0	0	69	**_1210_**
	2	5	10	11	12	13	14	15	16	22	**_1210_**
	605	242	121	110	101	93.1	86.4	80.7	76	55	
	1	1	1	1	0	0	0	0	0	1	
1	607	247	131	121	0	0	0	0	0	77	**_1184_**

For the second sheet the number 1210, in the top right corner is divided by the numbers 2, 5, 10, 11, 12, 13, 14, 15, 16 and 22 with the quotients shown in the second row. The numbers in the fourth row are the sum of the first three numbers in columns one through seven. The number 1184 is the sum 1+607+247+131+121+77.

2	5	10	11	12	22	***1210***
=ROUND($H42/B42,2)		=ROUND($H42/C42,2)		=ROUND($H42/D42,2)		
=ROUND($H42/E42,2)		=ROUND($H42/F42,2)		=ROUND($H42/G42,2)		
=IF(B43=INT(B43),1,0)		=IF(C43=INT(C43),1,0)		=IF(D43=INT(D43),1,0)		
=IF(E43=INT(E43),1,0)		=IF(F43=INT(F43),1,0)		=IF(G43=INT(G43),1,0)		
1 =B44*(B42+B43)		=C44*(C42+C43)		=D44*(D42+D43)		
=E44*(E42+E43)		=F44*(F42+F43)		=G44*(G42+G43)		***=SUM(A45:G45)***

Appendix E

The spreadsheet calculates the proper divisors 512, a powers of 2 as well as the sum of these proper divisors

512	2	4	8	16	32	64	128	256	512	1024	2048	
	1	1	1	1	1	1	1	1	0	0		
	1	1	1	1	1	1	1	1	0	1	1	SUM
1	2	4	8	16	32	64	128	256	0	0	0	511

512*2 =B26*2 =C26*2   =D26*2 =E26*2   =F26*2 =G26*2 =H26*2
=I26*2 =J26*2 =K26*2

=IF($A26/B26=INT($A26/B26),1,0)
=IF($A26/C26=INT($A26/C26),1,0)
=IF($A26/D26=INT($A26/D26),1,0)
=IF($A26/E26=INT($A26/E26),1,0)
=IF($A26/F26=INT($A26/F26),1,0)
=IF($A26/G26=INT($A26/G26),1,0)
=IF($A26/H26=INT($A26/H26),1,0)
=IF($A26/I26=INT($A26/I26),1,0)
=IF($A26/J26=INT($A26/J26),1,0)
=IF($A26/K26=INT($A26/K26),1,0)
=IF($A26/L26=INT($A26/L26),1,0)

=IF(B26=$A26,0,1)   =IF(C26=$A26,0,1)   =IF(D26=$A26,0,1)
=IF(E26=$A26,0,1)   =IF(F26=$A26,0,1)   =IF(G26=$A26,0,1)
=IF(H26=$A26,0,1)   =IF(I26=$A26,0,1)   =IF(J26=$A26,0,1)
=IF(K26=$A26,0,1)   =IF(L26=$A26,0,1)   SUM
    1   =B27*B28*B26 =C27*C28*C26 =D27*D28*D26 =E27*E28*E26

=F27*F28*F26

=G27*G28*G26 =H27*H28*H26 =I27*I28*I26 =J27*J28*J26
=K27*K28*K26 =L27*L28*L26   =SUM(A29:L29)

Appendix F

For Euclid's proof that there is no largest prime number, I will use subscript notation to represent the list of the assumed finite collection of prime numbers:

$P_1, P_2, P_3, P_4, \ldots, P_K, \ldots, P_L$, where $P_1=2$, $P_2=3$, $P_3=4$, $P_4=7$, etc.

Then P_K represents the Kth prime while P_L represents the assumed largest prime number. Euclid's number Q equals one plus the product of the assumed finite prime numbers, so $Q=1+P_1{}^*P_2{}^*P_3{}^*\ldots{}^*P_{K-1}{}^*P_K{}^*P_{K+1}{}^*\ldots{}^*P_{L-1}{}^*P_L$ is larger than every prime, and in particular is larger than the assumed largest prime, P_L. Because Q is not a prime number it must be divisible by a prime. We represent the prime divisor of Q as P_K, then $Q=P_K{}^*J$ for some number
J. So $1=Q- P_1{}^*P_2{}^*P_3{}^*\ldots{}^*P_{K-1}{}^*P_K{}^*P_{K+1}{}^*\ldots{}^*P_{L-1}{}^*P_L$
Substituting $P_K{}^*J$ for Q results in $1= P_K{}^*J-P_1{}^*P_2{}^*P_3{}^*\ldots{}^*P_{K-1}{}^*P_K{}^*P_{K+1}{}^*\ldots{}^*P_{L-1}{}^*P_L$
Factoring results in
$1= P_K{}^*J-P_K{}^*(P_1{}^*P_2{}^*P_3{}^*\ldots{}^*P_{K-1}{}^*P_{K+1}{}^*\ldots{}^*P_{L-1}{}^*P_L)$
This last equation is a contradiction to arithmetic because the number 1 is not divisible by the prime number P_K.

Appendix G

Dedekind – Peano Axiomatic Arithmetic.

Axiom 1: We assume a collection of undefined objects with at least one member and with a unary operation defined. The assumed object will be given the symbol 0. By a unary operation, we mean a process by which to each object in the collection, another object in the collection is assigned. Our unary operation will be pronounced SUCCESSOR and will be symbolized with the letter S. The SUCCESSOR of an object will be another object in the collection.

The symbol for equality is = and is defined by the properties we propose for it.

Axiom 2: For each object N in the collection, N=N (reflexive property of =.)

Axiom 3: For objects N and M in the collection, if N=M, then M=N (symmetric property of =.)

Axiom 4: For objects L, M, and N in the collection, if L=M and M=N, then L=N (transitive property of =.)

Axiom 5: For each object N in the collection, if N=M then M is also in the collection (closure under =.)

Axiom 6: For each object N in the collection, the SUCCESSOR of N, denoted S(N) is also in the collection (closure under SUCCESSOR.)

Axiom 7: For each object N in the collect, S(N)=0 is false (assuring a smallest object in the collection.)

Axiom 8: For objects N and M in the collection, if S(N)=S(M), then N=M (objects in the collection are unique.)

Axiom 9: If a statement is true for 0 and then true for S(N) as a result of being true for N, then the statement is true for every member of the collection (provides for inductive reasoning.)

The intention of the axioms is to reduce arithmetic to syntax and to reduce proof to logic applied to the syntax. Semantic interpretations can only suggest what might be true.

At this point we define some symbols that will ease the manipulation of $S(0)$, $S(S(0))$, $S(S(S(0)))$. We define $S(0)$ to be the symbol 1 and $S(S(0))$ to be the symbol 2. Since $S(0)=1$, $S(1)=S(S(0))=2$. We now have $S(S(S(0)))=S(S(1))=S(2)$ and define this to be the symbol 3. In this manner the count N of the SUCCESSORS defines our well known symbols (4, 5, 6, etc.).

We define a binary operation + for objects M and N, using two rules: Rule 1: $N+0=N$, Rule 2: $N+S(M)=S(N+M)$. We then have $0+0=0$ and $1+1=1+S(0)=S(1+0)=S(1)=2$. So $2+1=2+S(0)$ which equal $S(2+0)=S(2)=S(S(S(0)))=3$. Continuing this idea, $1+2=S[1+S(1)]=$

$S[1+S(S(0)]=S(S(S(0)))=3$. In general we have $S(M+N)=S(N+M)$ and $S[(L+M)+N]=S[L+(M+N)]$, the commutative and associative properties of addition respectively.

Peano and other mathematicians continued with definitions and notations and developed a theory of arithmetic which was a reasonable reflection of the arithmetic we use daily. Godel then showed that there will always be undecidable arithmetic propositions.

References

A History of Mathematics by Uta C. Merzbach and Carl B. Boyer, Third edition, 2011, John Wiley & Sons, Inc.

Men of Mathematics by E. T. Bell, 1937, Simon & Schuster

The Man Who Loved Only Numbers by Paul Hoffman, 1998, Hyperion

Elementary Number Theory by Gareth A. Jones and J. Mary Jones, 1998, Springer-Verlag

Mathematical Mysteries by CalvClawson, 1996, Basic Books

www.ingramcontent.com/pod-product-compliance
Lightning Source LLC
LaVergne TN
LVHW041536060526
838200LV00037B/1016